Earlier Reviews

There is discipline, spirit, no easy optimism, sensibility, and heart in these poems. ~Gary Snyder

To read *Adversaria* is to be in the presence of a lively and supple and various mind, as tough as it is American. ~Li-Young Lee

Russell, who works at Weirton Steel, knows how to pare language and image down to a crystal moment....The strength and straight-forwardness of these poems makes them some of the best statements on life not only in a steel mill but the small towns that surround it. ~Marianna Hofer

Tim Russell...is mining some of the same ore as Patchen, Wright, and more recently, Jim Daniels, but unlike those poets who write with the distance of time or persona, Russell writes, "In Medias Res," with an immediacy that is stunning and a knowledge of language and poetry that is accomplished.....Life goes on outside the factory, too, and throughout. Russell's son practices saxophone, the wistaria blooms, the slag heaps, feelings rise off the page. ~Diane Kendig

What Tim Russell knows best is being a family man in Toronto, Ohio, and a boilermaker across the river in Weirton Steel....If Russell feels exploited and abused, it is nowhere evident in these mostly serene poems. Like Dr. [William Carlos] Williams, he accepts his "local" for what it is....A surprising number of his poems are about nature—birds, trees, flowers, and animals—ethereally beautiful against the grim backdrop of a mill town. ~Fred Eckman

Ordinary objects, the 'bronze' baseball under forsythia bushes, the 'sopping' flag, the ore train clanking iambs and trochees, even the myriad changing faces of the river, are poignantly rendered. These are poems of the definite article. We do not see a crow, but 'the black black crow,' 'the robin perched atop the rusting flagpole.' Despite a pervasive decay and industrial blight, objects and people exhibit their own luminous integrity. ~Peter Blair

The genuineness and authority of Russell's work cannot be gainsaid; he brings us close to ordinary life, and then inside its strangeness. ~*Poetry*

The life that Russell portrays, hard as it is, is a whole life, awful and lovely. ~*Hudson Review*

Adversaria is a classy addition to the Rust Belt strain of the American grain. ~*Taproot Reviews*

Commentary

For some reason that still seems magical, Tim and I resonated. We were both intense. We had our eyes on language, on poetry as a pathway to salvation. But my devotion was that of a pious worshiper, of one wanting to escape the reality, the sick fact of the world, its Vietnams, its steel mills, its bullies, its general abuse of all things I thought deserved to be valued. Language, especially the *sotto voce* of it loomed as an enchanting escape for me. But Tim, with or without his MFA, in his pure genius, was a blacksmith who knew how to forge it, knew that the world, and all it encompassed was the ore that had to be parlayed, commerced, bent and twisted, smoothed and polished, burnished into poetry. ~Earl Keener

Timothy Russell's poetry alloys the grit of the Ohio Valley and the delicate brush strokes of Basho and Shiki, as only the white heat of a Weirton Steel blast furnace could do. Both lyric poet and "Mad Dog," Tim was and is the essential voice of the region while never being confined by its boundaries. Tim is a hidden master come here into the light. ~Valerie Nieman, author of *Leopard Lady: A Life in Verse*

In Plena Vita - The Full Life
Collected Poems

Timothy Russell

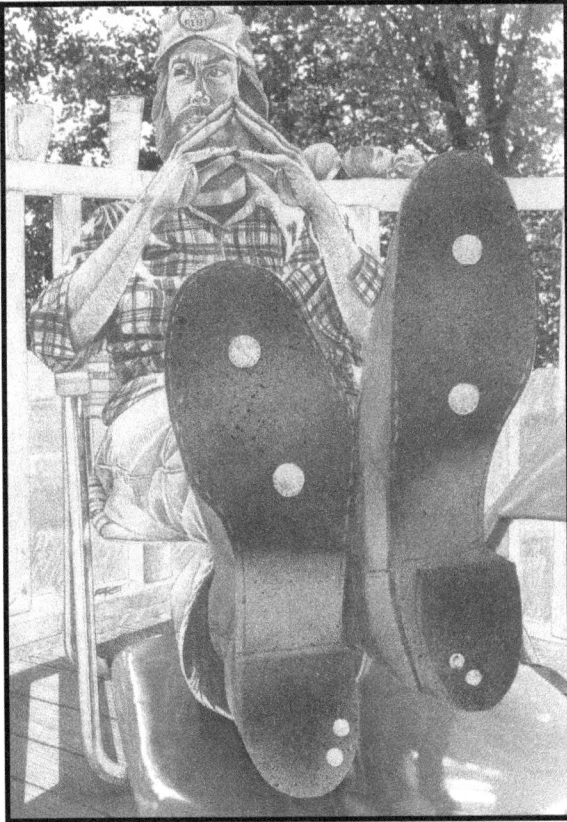

Edited by
Marc Harshman & Larry Smith
Assistant Editor Ivan Russell

Special Edition
Working Lives Series
Bottom Dog Press

Credits
Editors: Marc Harshman and Larry Smith
Assistant Editor: Ivan Russell
Cover Design: Susanna Sharp-Schwacke
Book Layout: Larry Smith
Cover Photo and Interior Photos: Jodi Dolan Russell
Art on Title Page: Steve Opet
Photo and Text Scanning: Ivan Russell
Chief copyeditor: Violet (Russell) Wender

Acknowledgments on page 272

**This is a signed limited edition
available only from Bottom Dog Press
& Jodi Russell**

**Bottom Dog Press
Huron, Ohio**

Table of Contents

~ Contents ~

The Possibility of Turning to Salt (Chapbook 1987)
(Ohio Poetry Association Golden Web Award)
Contents:

~ Contents ~

A Day Without Rain

In Dubio (Chapbook 1988)
(State Street Press Award)
Contents:

In Medias (Chapbook 1991)
Contents:

~ Contents ~

Adversaria (Book 1993)
(Terrence Des Pres Prize for Poetry, Tri-Quarterly Books)
Contents:

~ Contents ~

~ Contents ~

~ Contents ~

Other Poems—Selected (Post 1996)

Early Period

Middle Period

~ Contents ~

~ Contents ~

Timothy Russell Biographical Timeline
Prepared by Jodi Dolan Russell and Violet (Russell) Wender,
Ivan Russell, and Larry Smith

1951 – Timothy (Tim) is born in Steubenville, Ohio on May 25th, the eldest of Ruth (Roush) and Charlie Russell's six children. Charlie works as an accountant in the steel mill. Later, after Tim leaves home, Ruth becomes a grade school teacher and eventually a grade school principal. They are living in Follansbee, West Virginia, a small steel mill town along the Ohio River; also known as "Little Italy." In his youth, Tim serves as an altar boy in the Catholic Church.

1969 – Early winter, Tim is in a car accident needing 69 sutures to repair facial injuries. He works at a gas station in town, then the town's Pizza Inn restaurant. He graduates from Madonna High School in Weirton, West Virginia, where his English teacher Walter Wieloh recognizes his writing potential, and in subsequent years requests a poem from Tim for the student magazine, *The Trumpet*. Tim graduates that summer and meets Josephine (Jodi) Dolan in a Catholic church in Follansbee. She had come from New Jersey to West Virginia with Action Corps, a socialwork program designed to help Appalachian families then sponsored through the Catholic Church in the Diocese of Wheeling. They become friends. That fall he enters nearby West Liberty State College majoring in accounting. Jodi leaves West Virginia following a boy to Illinois.

1970 – A despondent Tim quits college to join the Army in January. He serves as a military police officer and sentry dog handler during the Viet Nam War. He declines an invitation to attend West Point Military Academy.

1971 – Tim receives a mournful letter from Jodi and drives to New Jersey in pursuit. They become engaged that May. He receives orders to go to Fort Carson, Colorado Springs, Colorado. In New Jersey on July 17th, they are married at On July 17th they are wed at Our Lady of Perpetual Help in Oakland, NJ. Jodi recalls, "We had a covered dish dinner reception at my parents' house. Tim wore sandals. I was pregnant and wore a wreath of flowers in my hair." Back in Colorado, Tim starts to write short stories, and Jodi develops her skills as a photographer.

~ Timeline ~

1972 - A son Shane is born in February. While in Colorado, they drive many miles on country roads in a new Ford Pinto, stopping at the tourist sites and antique shops along the way.

1973 – Tim becomes a sergeant, but decides to leave the Army with the promise of a job at Weirton Steel Company in Weirton, West Virginia. That December they move back to Follansbee where they live in a small house near his aunt, Angie Roush. Tim starts to send his stories and poems out to many magazines and contests.

1974 – They move to Weirton, buying their first house a few blocks from the Weirton Steel plant. Tim returns to West Liberty State College where Dr. William Sykes is so impressed with Tim's writing, he persuades him to change his major from accounting to English. This is a pivotal point in Tim's life, the start of his writing career. He also finds support in fellow author Peter Makuck.

That December their second son, Ivan, is born in Wheeling with birth complications, leading to a 10-day hospitalization at Weirton Medical Center. Tim is taking mid-semester tests, working full-time at the mill and driving Jodi to the hospital for breast feeding every 4 hours, day and night. (See "Love Poem" published in his 1987 chapbook *The Possibility of Turning to Salt*.)

1977 – Their third child, a daughter, Violet is born in Steubenville, Ohio, at the same hospital as her father. Tim graduates with a BA degree from West Liberty State College.

1979 – Over the next two years, while working full time at Weirton Steel in the blast furnace area and as a crane operator, Tim drives 40 miles to the University of Pittsburgh, graduating with a Master of Arts in English degree and a creative thesis "Under the Square Sky." Among his friends and fellow students are poets Lee-Young Li, Marc Harshman, Judith Vollmer, Peter Oresick, Kevin Rippin and Frank Lehner.

Early 80s – Tim joins the West Virginia Writers and begins attending their annual conference in Cedar Lakes, West Virginia, where over the years he wins many awards across different genres. He meets poet Allen Ginsberg there and becomes friends with fellow writers Earl Keener, and Val Nieman. Tim often shares work separately with his writer friends who continue to critique and encourage each other's writing until Tim's death. Tim completes a poetry manuscript, "Still Life."

Tim is diagnosed with lupus after having suffered the symptoms for a decade.

1982 – Their fourth child, a daughter Laurel, is born in Wheeling. For a time, Tim is laid off from Weirton Steel. He works at a tire shop in Richmond, Ohio, until being called back to the mill. He joins a writer's group in Weirton called John Hancock Writers Club run by Pam Markricosta and Jack Zierold.

1985 – Tim meets poet Jim Daniels at the *West Branch* annual writing festivals at Bucknell University. Tim will continue to attend for years afterward.

1987 – Chapbook *The Possibility of Turning to Salt* is published by the Ohio Poetry Day Association as their Golden Web Award winner.

1988 – Chapbook *In Dubio* receives the State Street Press Award, which includes publication.

1989 – On Halloween they move to a new house in Toronto, Ohio, along the bank of the Ohio River (Mile 60). The home was formerly owned by a doctor and boasts ten rooms. Tim finally has an office with a large desk in a semi-circular room built of brick and glass blocks.

1990 – Shane graduates from Toronto High School and joins the Army. Jodi begins working as a waitress and hostess, something she had not done since she was a teenager working in a New Jersey diner.

1991 – Tim is featured with three other steelworker poets in *A Red Shadows of Steel Mills* collection (Kip Knott, David Adams, and Richard Hague) published by Bottom Dog Press and launched at a group reading at Mac's Back's Books in Cleveland and Firelands College. He also has a chapbook *In Medias Res* published. Tim is known to fellow writers as "The Steel Mill Poet" and as "Mad Dog" by fellow workers from his antics of growling at orders. He presents a reading at Carnegie Mellon University thanks to poet-friend Jim Daniels.

1993 – *Adversaria*, Tim's first full length book, receives the Terrence Des Pres Prize for Poetry and is published by Tri-Quarterly Books. He travels the tri-state area (OH, WV, PA) promoting his book and giving readings. He reads at important places in his early writing career: West Liberty, the University of Pittsburgh, and Mary H. Weir Public Library, along with readings at universities, coffee shops, libraries, and bookstores. At one bookstore he reads in the front window as people pass by. Jodi recalls, "Tim even read in some bars, and it was great to hear people cheering and clinking glasses in appreciation."

On the advice of his doctor, Tim finally quits smoking. He chooses Violet's 16th birthday as his quit date. Ivan graduates from Toronto High School and after attending Kent State University joins the Army. Tim is diagnosed with cerebral vasculitis (a complication of his auto-immune disease) and given a poor prognosis. The University of Pittsburgh Medical Center is investigating an experimental chemotherapy treatment which cannot repair any prior damage to the brain but might halt its progression. Tim signs up for the research trial and receives Cytoxan, a potent chemotherapy drug. Luckily, it works for him and his prognosis improves with regards to the cerebral vasculitis. He continues to have symptoms associated with what doctors no longer believe is lupus, but instead "a lupus like syndrome."

1995 – Tim's chapbook *What We Don't Know Hurts* is published by Talent House Press. Violet graduates from Toronto High School and enrolls at Trinity Health System School of Nursing in Steubenville. Tim is interviewed by Dr. Stan Rubin of Brockport for the *Writers Forum* a celebrated series of broadcast interviews.

1996 – Tim and Jodi celebrate their 25th wedding anniversary at the American Legion Hall in Toronto. The party is held two days after Tim buries his mother. They had visited Ruth just a few days before she unexpectedly passed away. Jodi remembers that Ruth had made a tray of baklava for the anniversary party, and she had expressed happiness noting, "This will be like the wedding reception you two never had."

Tim receives the White Eagle Coffee House Press Award, including publication of the chapbook, *In Lacrimae* (1997).

1997 – Tim develops serious complications from long-term prednisone use. This medication causes fat deposits in unusual areas, the face, the abdomen, and in Tim's case his spinal column. Having already lost the sensation in his legs from his toes to the middle of his thighs, he must have surgery to remove the fatty deposits near his spine, or risk becoming permanently paralyzed. Five days after surgery, he develops a staph infection and has to have emergency surgery to his spine. During the second surgery they nick a nerve causing foot drop of his left foot which would later need corrective surgery. He never regains sensation in his legs despite the spinal surgery. He also develops Type 2 Diabetes and would often develop wounds on his feet that quickly became infected and often required intravenous antibiotics and hospital treatment stays.

1998 – Tim has four poems published in the esteemed *Poetry* magazine, which he regarded as a highlight as a writer.

Tim is forced to medically retire from Weirton Steel due to disability. The decades of having his auto-immune disorder had taken their toll. At times his muscles are affected, and he is too weak to hold his arms up to type. The cerebral vasculitis had also caused a change in his thinking process and writing becomes more challenging. This is around the time he begins to move from writing poetry back to writing haiku which he had first done in college. Jodi remembers Tim looking at haiku as a kind of word puzzle.

1999 – Tim is awarded the 4th Shiki International Haiku Award Shiki Team, Ehime Prefecture. The prize is a 10-day trip to Japan, which Tim records in a long travel *haiban,* a blend of prose and haiku entitled "japaniad."

Tim's father Charlie suffers a debilitating stroke from which he will not fully recover and will later live in Tim and Jodi's home where they will care for him until he is placed in a nursing home.

2000 – Laurel graduates from Toronto High School then later from Ohio University. Tim's health is getting progressively worse. His doctors compare his bone density to that of a 90-year-old woman. His doctors warn that lifting his dad and pushing him in his wheelchair put him at increased risk for spinal injury and he is advised to move Charlie into a nursing home. As Tim is pushing his dad's wheelchair into the nursing home, he feels a crack in his foot. He has severely fractured it and will himself be in a wheelchair for over a year.

2001 – Charlie passes away at 74, in the nursing home. Finding themselves in an empty home with no responsibility, Tim and Jodi do some limited international traveling to London and Paris.

2002 – Violet, knowing her dad had always wanted to visit Alaska, takes a travel nurse assignment in Anchorage. Tim flies out to stay with her for three weeks. Violet remembers, "We walked into a small coffee shop with a wall full of used books. He asked the owner if she'd give him a dollar if he found his book on the wall. She said sure. Then absolutely lost her composure when he actually found his book *Adversaria* in her store. She was delighted when he offered to sign the book."

2008 – In June, Tim is helping their sickly neighbor shovel slag because he is worried the neighbor might have a heart attack. As they are finishing up, Tim feels some pain in his left shoulder. He mentions this to Jodi, who suggests he go to the emergency room, but Tim chooses to wait for Violet's arrival. After hearing his symptons, she encourages him to go to the Emergency Department. At the Veteran's Hospital in Pittsburgh, PA, it is confirmed that he has had a heart attack. He needs to have a quadruple bypass, yet is hesitant to have his chest cracked open. Violet, pregnant, implores her dad to have surgery so that he could at least meet his first grandchild, and he agrees. Sophia Wender is born to Violet and David Wender, the first of 8 grandchildren.

2009 – Jodi begins commuting to Pittsburgh. Tim left home alone for the majority of days, cares for their dogs, keeps up with the yard work, pays the bills, and continues to write haiku and other poems. He begins collecting large stones from the banks of the Ohio river and creates a beautiful "Stonehenge" rock garden on their river bank property. "Years of hard work, sweat, bruises, and cuts go into its completion," recalls Jodi who fondly names it "Tim Henge." Here he grows poppies, zinnias, and sunflowers in its center. Jodi describes how "Battling knot weed on the hillside he turned it into a bird and wildlife sanctuary. He would ride along the banks of the river in his boat collecting garbage and debris trying to keep the river clean. He was mindful of sharing and taking care of the earth for everyone and everything." Tim is so physically active that after his bypass, his doctors are not worried when Tim refuses to go to cardiac rehab. Tim adopts the Japanese-style name of "Shachihoko" for his haiku submissions.

2011 – Tim and Jodi celebrate their 40th Anniversary with a party on their river property with family and friends. Tim continues to write, mostly in haiku form and publishing in over 50 international places.

2014 – 2019 He often sends poems to the members of his close family.

2020 – COVID-19 limits Tim and Jodi's interactions with others. His auto-immune disease makes it too risky to have visitors. Jodi stops working as a restaurant hostess, and Tim stays busy with yard work, maintaining Tim Henge area, and battling knotweed on the riverbank. In October Tim receives the devastating news that he has leukemia. He is told there was no cure, but there is some treatment that could prolong his time with us. Again he is hesitant, but Violet implores him to try "for the grandkids."

~ Timeline ~

2021 – July 17th marks the 50th anniversary for Tim and Jodi.
September 16th Tim dies at 70 years at his home after a fight with myelodysplastic syndrome (MDS preleukemia).
Tim's last haiku written a day before he dies:

Snoozles

the little dog knows

I'm toast –

2022 – May 21st part of Tim's ashes are buried at the National Cemetery of the Alleghenies, with military honors. July 30th Tim Russell Celebration of Life is conducted along the banks of the Ohio River with statements by friends and family. His ashes are spread on the river by his wife Jodi and their grandchildren.

Tim at Tim Henge site near their Toronto home, 2021

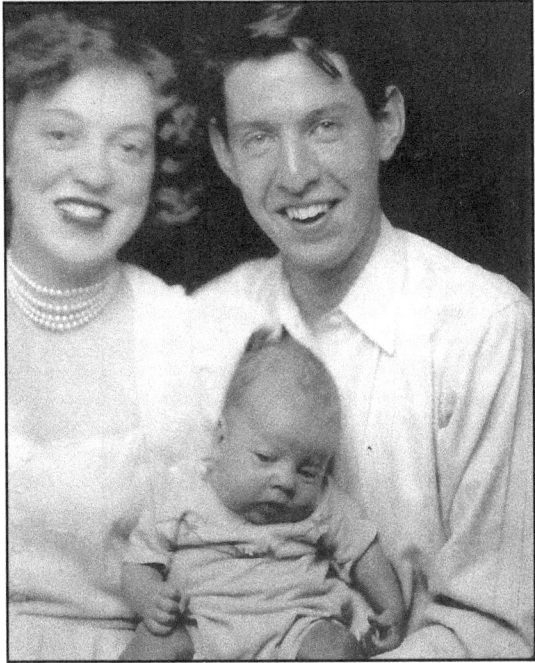

Infant Timothy with parents Ruth (Roush) and Charles Russell, b. May 25, 1951 Steubenville, Ohio

8th grade school photo
Follansbee Middle School

Graduation photo
from Madonna High School,
Weirton, WV 1970

Tim as dog trainer
with police dog Rufus,
Lackland Air Force Base,
Tx, 1970

~ Photos ~

Jodi and Tim's wedding party at home of
her parents in New Jersey, July 17, 1971

Tim, Jodi and their new Ford
Pinto en route to Fort
Carson, Colorado Springs,
where he is stationed, 1971

Tim and Jodi from
photo booth at
Kennywood Amusement Park,
Pittsburgh, 1978

Tim and Jodi at his graduation
from West Liberty State College
1974

Family photo: Jodi, Ivan, Tim, Shane living in Weirton, WV, 1976

Tim and Jodi with baby Laurel, 1982

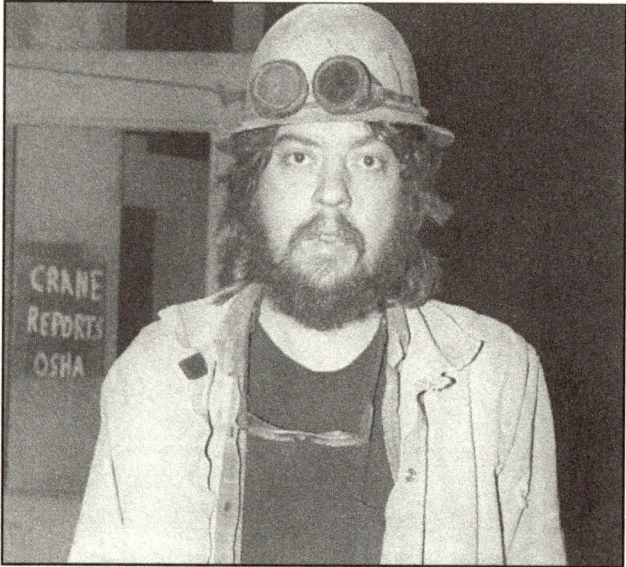

Tim working as an apprentice millright Weirton Steel Plant c. 1990 (photo by Steve Opet)

Tim at work cleaning up the Ohio River near his home in Toronto, OH, c. 2010

Pittsburgh Poetry Scene c.1980s
Standing left to right: Ed Ochester, Frank Lehner, Marilyn Keener,
Lee Ann Setlack, Kristen Kovacic, Brit Ochester. Seated:
Jim Daniels, Kevin Rippin, Nancy Koerbel, Timothy Russell, Earl Keener

Marc Harshman, Tim and Jodi near Russell home in Toronto, 2020

Tim and Jodi on trip to Paris, in photo booth 2001

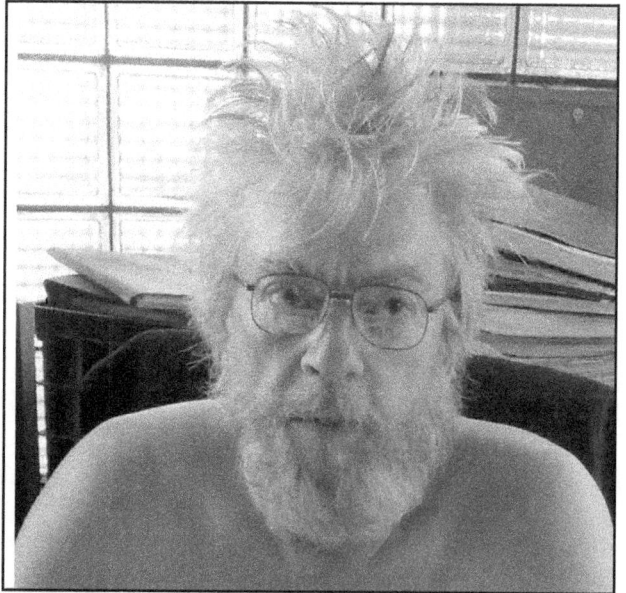

Tim at work in home office, Toronto, Ohio, c. 2020

~ Photos ~

Tim on 10-day trip to
Matsuyama Japan,
winner of the Shiki Award,
1999

Tim and Violet,
Girdwood, Alaska,
2002

Tim and Jodi at
son Shane's wedding party, 2015

Tim Henge site built by Tim along the Ohio River

Introduction by Marc Harshman

An unwavering devotion to truth, both uplifting and sober-
ing, is the hallmark of Timothy Russell's extraordinary writing. In
poem after poem, he finds both beauty and sustenance in the harsh
circumstances of living and working in the gritty factory towns of
the upper Ohio Valley of West Virginia and Ohio. Just as the clouds
of mill smoke enveloped much of his life, the presence of the steel
mills themselves undergird many of his poems. Additionally, al-
though Russell is never less than a faithful witness to the oppressive
and sometimes brutal realities of this region, he seems possessed,
always, of a fierce desire to illumine the light within the dark. It is
this desire which most distinguishes these fine poems.

The topics of the factory and the river, the blue-collar liveli-
hoods of his neighbors, and the common flora of the yards and the
steep hills beyond, his ailanthus and spruce, clematis and forsythia, all
uniquely inform the idiosyncratic and distinctive voice I've come to
recognize as uniquely Russell's and his alone. Philip Levine, Richard
Hugo, Marge Piercy and, though it may seem odd to say, even Lorine
Niedecker come to mind. With Niedecker I'm thinking of the suc-
cinct precision Russell brings to bear in his best work.

Of course, there is also James Wright. Anyone who writes
from the upper Ohio Valley and the tri-state region of West Virginia,
Pennsylvania, and Ohio works under Wright's shadow. Russell's rela-
tionship to Wright seems to me a subtle one. He seldom mentions
Wright in his work. There is his poem, *On Reading the Collected Works
of the One Good Poet from Martins Ferry, Ohio,* which is great fun but
more of a parody in tribute. I do, however, fondly recall conversa-
tions where we both talked with awe of certain of Wright's more
iconic poems like *Lying in a Hammock…* and *A Blessing,* curiously nei-
ther of which are among Wright's Ohio Valley poems. But if I had
to trace an influence of Wright upon Russell, I'd say it was simply
what we all treasure when we discover we've been given permission
to write about our very own place, warts and all.

Beyond that, Russell, like Wright, had acute observational skills that allowed the creation of superb images like "an electrical storm / of recognition struck / me..." from *In Passim* or these opening lines from *In Promptu*:

The coral sun presides
over the swollen horizon
beyond the dowager magnolia.

Timothy Russell is easily one of the most overlooked poetic voices not only in Appalachia but in America. He's overlooked in Appalachia, in part, because of geography, raised as he was toward the northern boundary of the region where the backdrop for many of his poems is the industrial melting pot of cities like Wheeling, West Virginia, Steubenville, Ohio, and Pittsburgh, Pennsylvania. And although these may not seem Appalachian to some, the people who live here share nearly all the same characteristics as their rural and more southern cousins in being hard-working, fiercely loyal to neighbor and family, and self-reliant. His particular cities were Follansbee and Weirton, West Virginia where he was raised and their cross-river twins: Steubenville his birth place and Toronto where came to reside.

Russell is too often overlooked nationally because, although he wins the prestigious Terrence Des Pres Prize from *Tri Quarterly Press* [Chicago] in 1993, within the following decade he begins to fall victim to a heart-breaking array of debilitating illnesses that gradually curtail his energy and thus his output. With this in mind, I can now better understand how the wider circulation of Russell's poems was limited to a relatively few years. With illness there came concentration issues that led him to the short, condensed form of the haiku. This is not a complaint—his haiku are arresting and stunningly beautiful. That he turned to the haiku is simply an observation, perhaps a partial explanation of the changes that can be observed in his later work. And make no mistake, with his haiku his brilliant poetic skills continued as clearly shown by his winning the 4th Shiki International Haiku Award in 1999, an award that would bring about a trip to Japan. This same trip would lead him to create a masterful account of his travels through the use of the haibun, a poetic formula combining haiku with prose commentary.

~Introduction~

To open a talk regarding poets of northern Appalachia at a past Appalachian Studies Association conference I read these words from Russell's poem *In Plano*.

> Because hills are not on the maps,
> it's easy to get lost here, distant
> neighborhoods appear to be adjacent.

I find these particular lines very insightful. Even though I have lived my adult life in West Virginia and a decade of those in a prototypically rural Appalachian neighborhood, I find these words ring true for both the rural and the urban places of Appalachia. And it is, indeed, "easy to get lost here," whether on the isolated ridge called Sally's Backbone where I once lived or Tim's mill towns, his poems seem always to be pointing a way, providing an anchor, enabling us, his readers, to feel just a little bit less lost. That's a gift, a gift worth remembering and which only the finest poets offer.

I first met Tim through our enrollment in what was for me the still fledgling MFA program at University of Pittsburgh. Although two years behind me in the program, I immediately sensed in Tim a colleague who was more than a peer, wiser than most including some professors, and I soon saw, too, that he was crafting poems not only with his mind but with the true sweat of the heart, poems honed with an honesty that put most of the rest of our embarrassingly meager work to shame.

He was a big man, physically, and perhaps that somehow fed the size of his presence which also seemed big. Tim spoke. I listened. I think we all did. Myself, I was so gun-shy of everyone in those days that I might never have claimed him as a friend except that soon, thankfully, through some weird alignment of the stars, we became more than colleagues, we did become friends. I learned how to catch that wry glint of his eye that bespoke some brisk humorous anecdote on its way.

A mill worker for over twenty years, few poets capture, as I've already intimated, the experience of place and work as does Russell. I've also already mentioned Philip Levine and others in whose company Russell would be comfortable. From his first poem in his chapbook *In Dubio* where "men tend machinery all night / as if it were troubled livestock," to his *In Consideratione Praemissourum* where stupefied from work, "Seven men on a railroad tie" share thoughts of home, their "down hoopy," and then inexplicably "... know their lunch break is over." That "know" is a very knowing *know*, one lived from the inside out by a man who has sat on that same railroad tie, who knew what it meant to be "dazed" by work.

That he was also such a remarkable poet is the wonder and the larger gift. Personally, I used to think first of all these poems that deliver such discerning attention, as well as give such unflinching witness to what were his twenty plus years of work in the steel mill. As we gathered this volume, however, I was startled to find there were nearly as many poems concerning domestic matters quite divorced from the world of work, poems of the everyday within which beauty of so many kinds was marvelously voiced. Poem after poem are bursting with aesthetic charm and with such restraint that they still take my breath away every time I read them. His account of the turning of the monthly seasons in *In Adversa* with its nuthatch "skittering head-first / down the bare black walnut" to his putting on of a "white shirt" in the poem *In Itegrum* to "celebrate my neighbor's glaring roof" with its "nest of black branches above it..." remind me of how hyper-attentive Russell was to the minutiae of every moment and object of life surrounding him.

Another striking feature of Russell's work is that despite the precision of detail at work in so many of his poems, he never gives away the mystery easily, but rather forces the reader to read beyond the poem, to reach beyond any quick conclusion. Or as Gary Snyder said regarding Russell's early work: "There is discipline, spirit, no easy optimism, sensibility, heart in these poems." In the long poem *In Actu*, Russell observes with a precise naming what appears in his field of vision as he looks out from his home across neighborhood and workplace. However, just as I think the poem will somehow celebrate the poet's place, the narrator turns away, declares that "all of it below me, behind me, / vanishes." Moreover, the poem goes on: "Everything disappears— / until somebody else who lives there, / or works there, on the railroads, say, / comes along to retrieve it."

The spirit of Whitman is very much at work in that poem but even more so in other poems like *In His Verbis* where Russell's vision becomes a mad rushing forth of metaphor with his repetition of the word "how," that word pushing forward the narrative: "<u>How</u> the thunderstorm was a mad scenario…" "<u>How</u> there is failure in these words. And plague." [my underlines]. Whitman named the world as he saw it. Russell names the world twice, simultaneously as what it is and what it can be imagined from the inner soul.

Elsewhere though, Russell is just as easily at home as a storyteller telling the stories of his family, neighbors, and co-workers. *In Aequo Animo* provides another instance of the unexpected twist Russell invariably provides in so many of his poems. Here he tells us of a late night traffic run to fix a pilot light at his parent's home only to suddenly shine the harsh light of their mortal futures upon the final lines. Or in a simpler vein Russell can effortlessly tell of the erotic moments within the round of familial life as in *In Bono Et Malo* where she "lowers the straps / of her orange nightgown, / and smiles, wickedly." And in certain poems like *In Exitu* Russell excels in melding his microscopic attention to detail with a heart-rending vision of the stories within the peopled world around him, in this instance of the "retarded boy" who has fallen on the hillside amidst a flurry of seemingly unrelated details that grow to underscore the pathos and transformation of the revealed circumstances. I sometimes think it's as if Russell takes Williams' "red wheelbarrow" and shows with storied detail how so much really does "depend upon…"

There are other poems less easily classifiable, poems that although they contain Russell's ever present sense of place, it's place seen from the inside first: "You'd like to believe all the places / you've ever lived are never vacant, / and Hansel and Gretel still manage / a candy story in Greensburg, Pennsylvania…" he writes in *You'd Like to Believe* where you come to realize his opening rumination about his very real mortality depends upon both the situations and places he most imagines believable but only if "someone will know." Hard not to think of Jack Gilbert when reading poems like this where Russell's imagination marries an almost surreal vision with the concrete details of the personal.

Like the American painters Sheeler and Demuth, or the composer Charles Ives, or poets like those already named, as well as others like Jim Daniels and Dorianne Laux, Russell had the uncanny ability of transforming the everyday world of labor and dirt, sweat and hard times into rare and memorable beauty. Timothy Russell and his poems, late though it may be, should join the top ranks of blue-collar poets revered around the world. We need such humbling, articulate, and loving voices now more than ever.

~ *Marc Harshman*, Poet Laureate of West Virginia (April 2023)

Publisher's Note

This book could not have come about without the devoted work of Timothy Russell's family. First of all, his wife Jodi who, with son Ivan, gathered the hundreds of poems and photos from Tim's boxes, drawers, folders and files. Ivan assisted as the finder and scanner of these many sheets, sometimes having to iron out the papers on which they were written. He was aided early on by Frank Lehner, Nancy Koerbel, Valerie Niemann and Kevin Rippin. Tim's Daughter Violet (Russell) Wender assisted in the research and writing of the Timeline and "Remembrance." Most of all, we are indebted to Tim himself who kept up the writing and printing out of these poems. His record of submissions and publications in a panorama of independent small and literary magazines rivals all others. Know that he did keep records and did foresee a collection such as this. Tim's friends and fellow poets kept the project going by offering insights to the man and the work. We are indebted to Marc Harshman who put in countless hours of devoted reading and editing of the manuscript and for his fine introduction. This is a "collected" work in chronological order, yet there is more to come of Tim's haiku and prose.

I and Bottom Dog Press are honored to carry the work of Timothy Russell forward to an ever-expanding audience of readers. More than a working-class and nature poet, he is a poet of our collective humanity.

~*Larry Smith,* editor of Bottom Dog Press (April 2023)

Here

Old women with emphysema
sleep in black
enameled rocking chairs
imported by the dozens
many years ago
before the fruit changed colors
inside the Mason jars downstairs,
before the times went rotten.
Here women like Anna,
past eighty, turn their gardens
every spring and plant
soft peaches in neat rows.
Every fall they cut the saplings,
bundle them neatly with rags,
and let the trash men take them.

Something's on Fire

I can't see anything clearly
beyond the swaybacked roof
of my neighbor's house,
but I heard sirens earlier,
and smoke is drifting slowly
following the mill buildings'
black roofs up the valley.
The droning hasn't stopped,
and I can hear them driving
pilings at the filtration site,
so it must not be too serious.
I'll probably hear about it
Monday when I go back to work.

The Porch and the Sycamore

The porch is so near
the sycamore,
its paint peels
exactly like bark.

I don't understand
why the porch has no steps
but the tree has five
spiked to it.

It's got something to do
with the porch being stuck
high on the back of the house
and sagging with its own weight,

while the tree grows and grows.
Whoever lived here before me
wanted to cut the tree
but propped the porch up.

If I could graft the porch
to the sycamore,
I'd forget about paint
and sit in the tree.

Nothing to Worry About

It's early yet. One of my sons
picked a bunch of pink flowers
and put them on my desk
in a glass with several fish
painted on it. It's been a week
now and not one green leaf
has browned, not one petal
has fallen off or even curled,
though there is a sprinkling of yellow pollen
in the dust. I want to thank him
before I forget, but he is sleeping.
Suddenly, I must go and bend
close to him, not to kiss
his forehead or to adjust
his blanket, but to hear
his breathing, and then
it's the others, his sister
and brother. Nothing else
is important. They are, of course, alive.
There's nothing to worry about,
but I still can't sleep.
I think of my friend
who was tending new shoots
of bamboo behind his house
when an arrow struck the ground
exactly between his hands
as if he had reached for it.
He said it startled him so much
he couldn't cry out.
He told me his daughter is fine,
cooking again, preparing blood
at a hospital in Richmond.

He told me her neck has healed;
they've taken the screws out of her skull
and removed the halo-brace.
Next week, I want to stop
the newspaper. Listen to this:

SAN DIEGO—Ghoulish looters
scurried into the burning wreckage
to rob the dead. They stripped bodies
of their money and jewelry.

It must have something to do with survival.
There's nothing to worry about
except the sycamore that's twice
as high as the house.
I went up higher than my chimney
to lop off a few limbs.
Dizziness at fifty feet
is thrilling but the nausea is scary.
I still have the scrapes on my arms
and legs and chest from hugging
so hard. I felt so old
I wanted to let go.
Even when I do sleep, flies buzz me awake.
I saw a mosquito flexing her legs
against the ceiling
while she digested the sweet juice
of my eyelid. When I swat
at flies with a magazine,
I see what keeps them alive.
They're nervous as convicts
all ways fidgety, unpredictable.

Love Poem

I remember pumping milk
from your breasts
with plastic baby-bottles
while Ivan slept blindfolded
under ultraviolet light
for the jaundice
which was nothing
but a minor complication.
I know you prayed for him
to get a sudden case of diarrhea
so we would know
there was no chance of gangrene
in his intestines.
You went to the hospital
every four hours to feed him
to inspect him [first]
for the least sign of passage.
The nurses said you needed sleep.
They were right. But they were wrong
about your having to stop nursing.
For his two o'clock feedings
you pumped the milk yourself
with those plastic bottles
because the nurses
with impregnable argument
said *no* to the breast pump,
and when you just couldn't do it
anymore because your hand shook
as the ragged lip
of the sterile mouth
closed around your raw nipple,
I had to help you

by taking the bottle
in my clumsy hand
while you closed your eyes
concentrating on the pain
and refusing to witness
the unnatural act yet again,
but imagining the mouth
of the baby at your breast.
I watched your nipple extend itself
inside the milky plastic,
and felt the bottle slowly warm
as it filled.
Sometimes I wake up
thinking I've dreamed us
older than we are and we still
live over the chocolate shop
with that awful siren near
that made us shudder
and cling together
as if our lives were in danger.
You scared me this morning
when you told me I fell
out of bed last night
without waking. I don't remember
you touching my arm
or calling my name.
And when you said
my skin was so cold
you thought I was dead
it terrified me.
I remember tasting your milk,
drinking some from a cup.
It was so warm and sweet,
it was hard to swallow.

Yellow Jacket

My son steps carefully
as a drunkard on a line.
The miniature jockey
riding his balanced thumb
is a yellow jacket
flexing its abdomen.
There's nothing I can do
but see what he shows me:
twitching mica wings,
sunlight imprisoned
in transparent veins.
He will survive me,
this small boy.

The Thaw Next Spring

A drift out back shrinks,
and a boot slowly kicks out
by degrees a clean black sole
smooth as an ankle bone.
No one recognizes it.
No one stops to claim it.
During the night peeling fingers
dig through the crust.
Next day sycamore branches
come to the surface
and a bruised hand
with five or six coins in it.

I Was Just Watching

I was just watching an ant
dragging the metallic corpse
of a fly along the curb,
the coppery back plate
and green abdomen both shining,
like an eye skidding across
a small piece of river gravel
jutting from the worn concrete.
The tiny red ant had hold
of a facial appendage,
perhaps a part of the mouth
in a posthumous kiss.
The fly tipped over, then
like an early flying machine,
the ant hanging on
like a deluded pilot
feet wildly pedaling the air.
The ant finally landed,
though, and immediately
renewed its struggle
backing into a tiny cluster
of seeds I would never have noticed.

Grasshoppers

They make good bait.

You can hear them
flicking their legs
inside the coffee can,
fifteen or eighteen of them
all trying to get out.

The steel point going in
makes the grasshopper
look bigger.
I string them together
with a sewing needle and thread.

They live a long time.

On Reading the Collected Works of the One Good Poet from Martins Ferry, Ohio

I've never dreamed
of being a horse before,
never even seen one
(Maybe they've all fled
to the white-boned fields
of Minnesota),
never seen one
stop to drink
from the Ohio's sludge.
Slag heaps higher
than you ever saw
still pyramid
to the red sky,
and high school sons
still gallop fiercely
up and down the valley.
Here men still die
of too much coal
or too much steel
or too many dreams,
but you have to be born
to want to be a horse
the way you have
to be born to live
near the oldest whorehouse
in Wheeling, West Virginia.

To a Younger Brother

Here is some broken glass
for you to swallow
or grind into your eyes.
You'd never say that.
I'm the extreme one,
after all this time still looking
for limits. You were always
the settler, not the explorer.
When I got tired of letting
Phil Siccurella beat me
every day because I was afraid
of hurting him, I decided
to kill him. So it was
I grabbed his neck and slammed his head
against the asphalt in the alley
again and again—I don't know
how many times, until I thought
he had to be dead. And so it was
we became friends. You could never
kill somebody, could you?
You tried to kill me
a couple years later
when you shoved me out of the tree house.
You show that damned scar
on your finger to anybody and say
your brother did that to you
with a hatchet. That was twenty years ago.
I should've cut it off
so you couldn't show it to anybody.
But it was an accident. You know that.
You could've lied about the scar,
told your friends it was glass,

a football injury, and not
your brother's hatchet.
I gave my second son
part of your name
because I loved you.
I'm sorry.

Obelisks

The Follansbee Area Municipal Park's
four-sided, pyramid-capped towers
built of stone and mortar
in a great depression on the side of a hill
still has obelisks skirting it,
wrist-thick chains hanging between them
like slack jump ropes.
Think of cemetery entrance pillars.
Think of Cleopatra's Needles,
one in London's sky, the other in Central Park's.
Think of the white monument to Washington.
Think of ascending inside the highest one,
the oldest one,
each step a stair trod to concavity,
of trudging up each flight
gravity increasing illogically,
of racing round and round
like a swallow in a silo,
of overtaking those on the flight above
or shuffling backward to the flight below,
of accomplishing a landing,
of resting between flights,
of struggling to convince your calf muscles to continue,
of enduring the stink of your own sweat,
of finally opening a door,
the small white door at the top.
Think of the buffeting wind.
Think of the obelisk swaying beneath you.
Think of the view.
Jump.

Four Rooms and a Bath

Am I moving my family
out of my heart
because they need a bigger place?

The Idea of Ambush

You have the idea of ambush
lodged in the plusher wing
of your brain's hotel

safely separated from those tourists,
your more common ideas,
who might disturb her vigil.

She sleeps with no one
and with one eye open
if she sleeps at all.

She smokes cheroots and spits
in the corner. Her presence
confuses you a little.

Is she waiting
for something to happen
once and for all

or does whatever it's going to be
depend on her as she
deftly taps a shell

into the well-oiled chamber?

The Margin for Error

The scenery here is unimpressive.
Mud under the catalpa
or the sycamore is gray

as an old snow tread
abandoned for years in somebody's garage,
useless.

This is a region
where everything is inexact,
where nothing matters

where it takes rain
to suppress the smell of creosote.

Geographically
the margin for error is bounded
on all sides

yet almost coincides with tolerance,
the way a confused system of roots
will fill the clay pot.

Vigilance

The swing creaks under me, although I'm still.

My knee warns me before every storm,
and it's easy to say the flickering there is

lightning or the same strain the swing resents,
but impossible to recall now that fury is gone,
the thunder, distant the lightning occasional,
the rain remains streaming on the pavement,

and I know swirling in the downspout.

I wonder how long all this water will take
by its undeniable logic to find the Ohio.

A small plane escaping the storm approaches,
and if the pilot were anybody but some Bogart,
I'd want to talk him safely down.

The engine falters but resumes its rhythmic stutter.

Bogie bound for the west unaware, I'm here watching,
not even a blip on his screen,
thinking the whole time he passes overhead
something is on the verge of finally happening.

Once I would've said *give me enough kindling*
and I'll set the world on fire,

but bravado recedes like so much thunder.
I'm only a man sitting on a porch swing
waiting and listening for something.

The Paprika Girl

Nobody can remember how to say
the name of the Paprika girl
whose breasts are pressed
against the cold linoleum
in somebody's dark kitchen,
her chin holding the sandwich
of her hands to the floor,
her ankles crossed. For once
she is naked voluntarily
and she makes faces at the baby
sitting otherwise ignored
on the living room floor,
while its parents and half its
grandparents finger their spots,
wiggle a shoe in vague discomfort,
and absently gaze at the imitation
bronze lamp's melancholy lovers.

Somebody will finally discover
the Paprika girl in the kitchen.
Perhaps the grandfather will notice
the engaged baby and the quizzical cock
of its head and he will get up
remembering the unlocked screen door
to investigate the source
of the baby's amusement.
The Paprika girl will lose
the baby's interest then and know
somebody's coming, and she will wave
to the baby as she gets up to run
slapping the screen door open
into the wheezing cicada darkness.

~ Still Life ~

Nobody can remember how to say
her name, but they know who she is
and when they return to the living room,
now and from now on,
even when the baby is grown,
they will have something to talk about—
that Paprika girl, or whatever
her name, who ran outside naked.

The Beginning of Amnesia

You have the feeling something is about
to finally happen tonight. Something inside
the wet signal box on the corner grinds
but doesn't catch. Whatever it is in there
discontinues its mindless function
to blend traffic intermittently
to break the flow into increments,
and the red stain on the black pavement
remains red. Someone has lost a lot
of crushed glass in the rain. You wait
for something you know must happen
but does not. There's no relief
from the shining street's red sparkle.
All you can see or remember or know
is the miniature electrified rash,
thousands of tiny beacons relaying
a single endless garbled message.

Suspended Animation

We've had several reports,
one of a small plane barely nicking
the Market Street Bridge
and cartwheeling into the Ohio,

another of perfectly circular leaves
sprouting overnight in a tulip tree,
and one of a beautiful woman wanting
to volunteer as a victim-at-large,

but nothing has been proven,
nothing has proven remarkable.
Everybody here wants something
to happen and to happen soon

I guess so whatever it is can be
reported or recorded or both
or condensed or exaggerated
or whatever it is that needs

to be done with it.
Witnessed I believe it is.
We are still quietly waiting,
but we are slowly becoming desperate.

The Invisible Bridge

If you are vaguely uneasy
because the bridge's ten pale lights cast
ten amber stains onto the black rippled surface,

because the man's body bobs adrift
bloated and grinning like a Macy's balloon,

or because the sparkling shapes always approach you
no matter where you are on the river,
characterizing the distance
between you and the invisible bridge
by never quite reaching you,

and if you know paint stiffened the sane
man's brush a month ago while he watched
bees pinning wisteria leaves in place

on the sagging trellis below him,
while he felt the aluminum ladder,
transmitting the slight vibrations
of his pulse to the damp sod,

you will ask yourself how a man
sensible enough to pause so long
in the chore of painting his home
came to be in the river or how

one small event invariably leads to another.

You'd Like to Believe

It's going to be your heart,
but you'd like to believe
you're disregarding the first slight tremors,
ignoring the first whispered rumors
of that desperately final revolt.
You'd like to believe you will not die
at the hands of some bitterly confused maniac,
or at the scene of some blunt accident.
You'd like to believe all the places
you've ever lived are never vacant,
and Hansel and Gretel still manage
a candy store in Greensburg, Pennsylvania,
and whoever lives above that confectionery
now puts the bed you left behind
to hard and regular use for love
and sleep, and you'd like to believe
somebody paused this morning and noticed
how the cottonwood outside a certain kitchen
in Fountain, Colorado, held the same
golden mountain you once saw in those branches.
You'd like to believe somebody else
has set foot in a white world,
horizonless and perfectly white,
white trees hovering over white rocks,
the air itself white,
everything on that mountainside
either frozen or snow-laden
and in the purest fog,
and you'd like to believe the sun
was not so small and white that morning.
You'd like to believe it was your heart
your first mate reeled in and left

to flop around on the deck of your marriage
in its pitifully slow suffocation.
You'd even like to believe you'd like to believe.
You'd like to believe you've been somewhere
through something and you'd like to believe
someone will know.

A Day Without Rain

A residue remains
on the windshield,
a tangled mass of silk
where the spider,
wind-borne this morning,
its underbelly tinted,
landed then struggled
as the wiper scraped
across the dry glass.
All day I mistook the smudge
for something on the horizon.

Even If It's Wrong

A man gets to thinking when he spends
too much time out in the sun
watching everything he knows,
his family and the place he loves,
slowly getting all the juice baked out of it
and he gets hold of something
when he's concentrating on how thirsty he is

and how afraid as his eyesight dries up,
and how he mourns the loss of sweat,
and how he knows the stones and few trees
are all cooking and heated through to their hearts,
and how he would give anything he has
to have all the water he could ask for,
anything to be caught in the rain,

and how everyone he knows is praying for it,
and how he wonders why his God would do this,
and he decides he's not going to sit idle
but he's going to pick up a hammer
and do something in preparation.
Now I don't *know* that it's going to rain,

but I believe it will, and I believe
that when it finally does, it won't stop,
not for a good long while.
Nobody knows what's going to happen,
but it stands to reason something will.

Throwing Things to the Flood

Since you left, I've collected
these things to throw
into the creek this spring:
this old photograph
of concrete blocks,
and you with a dandelion
in your mouth,
half an envelope
with a wavering cancellation
across some president's face,
and half an address
which about describes
the state of our union,
two snow tires
that will fit your car,
a laceless sneaker,
its tongue permanently wrinkled,
the porch swing
with its eight layers of paint,
all these ballpoint pens
and the cottage cheese
container you kept them in,
five cardboard boxes
full of the clothes
you didn't take with you,
and your pillow.
If you want to save anything,
come around before the rains.

The Still Life

He dozed under a galvanized roof
ignoring the hornets conferring in the rafters
over some emergency, possibly the still life himself,
possibly the sudden rain, and slept so contentedly
in that shed, sweat trickling from his temple
and exploring one of his ribs, he dreamed
all his earlier, more active days.

The rain stopped while he slept,
and started again, enough times to leach the zinc
from the corrugation, enough times for rust
to flourish. If he could have seen
the roof above, he would have recognized it
as a rippled negative impression of the sky
as it had been the day he was first born
and again the hour he first entered the shed.

Once and for All

He says he was trying to change
a blown fuse when he got his head
caught in the damned glove
compartment and that one jerk
hurt him worse than eating
barbed wire, but *no* he says
just when you start to believe him.
He was in a beer garden
with a woman he loved more than his
own eyes when she suddenly got hot
enough for no reason to pop
corn and raked a broken bottle
down across his nose
hurting him worse than a shoe
full of glass on a long hike,
but the truth is, he didn't
feel a thing chasing that ambulance,
then hearing water splashing
cold on a flat rock.
The water wasn't cold.
It was warm and it wasn't water.
It was blood emptying out of his head
right through his face.
Trouble is he says
he can't remember anything anymore
and has the scars to prove it.

The Pursuit of Happiness

You could say she displayed a lot of patience
appropriating for two weeks the slow blush
of a ripening fruit, either apple or peach,
and they'd never have found her if one hadn't
by cursing her name startled her into dropping
from her twig into the fast and cold water
where she became a sudden silvery trout
flashing downstream.

She avoided all their lures for so long
they were sure she was hungry and exhausted
when someone noticed a stepping-stone
snoring in mid-stream and planted his boot on it.
The stone grunted.

They got their hands on her then,
even as she sprouted head-legs-tail
and the black and gold symmetry on her back,
but while one of them was carrying her
beautiful reptile she erupted in flame and streaked
into the sky.

They're all old now, but they think of her
every time it rains.

The Possibility of Turning to Salt

It was impossible to sleep there,
not a level spot in the whole hundred and fifty acres
except the kitchen table wobbling so violently
we were afraid it might bolt for the woods,
which is what we did when we went there
isn't it? No electricity no gas, no phone,
no international papers for a while, no world
and no news of its absence. By Sunday morning
I was convinced some tick had burrowed
into my skull and was gorging itself. My whole brain
ached from the damage which, of course, was irreversible
and terminal. I was terrified already though
at what we'd said on Saturday that
moss in those woods was thick as carpet,
and that tanagers there were merely sparrows
who had flown through metallic paint,
and now I'm afraid the next time the world ends
it will kill me remembering what the world was like—
the sudden overdose of all that peace and quiet,
the withdrawal headache, the looking over my shoulder.

Ode to Posterity

The crack of a whip is no more than its tip
suddenly breaking the sound barrier.

It's the kind of information used as filler
at the bottom of a column of newsprint
like a shim or as a token buffer between
the bridal announcement and the stork notes.
When the crack of a whip is as brief
as a human life, how can you expect me
to gently cast you out with mere words,
then yank you back without snapping your spine
so violently your head pops off the instant
you see the inside of your private little sonic boom?

I cannot give you a line of words
that will snap back on themselves
for your sudden astonishment.
All I can do is give you words, words
like ingredients for a magical potion
or perhaps a nutritious stew,
add a catalyst or two and a waning and know
it is the trivial fact that you will remember,
that sound of the crack of a whip.

Biding Time

You never expected this,
the plot refusing to thicken,
the truck driver slapping his maroon beret
against his knee and saying, A*t least with him*
she didn't have to bury her heels in her ears
to get some honest penetration. Is that it?

You want to abandon the idea of ambush
and question your faith in static electricity.

Maybe you have missed something,
whatever it was you were sure was imminent.
Your body aches and twitches and ages

without your consent. How long you wonder
can you endure this simmering? You heard
the oldest board member denying the church
a chandelier for three reasons:

Nobody can spell well enough to order one,
probably nobody in the congregation can play one anyway,
and the back of the church is so dark
everybody ought to think about getting more light.

You ignore the whispered promise of a dancer
in nothing but smoky light in red spike heels
and so spent midnight in your kitchen watching
your neighbor's son practicing his debauchery
in the flash of his television's artificial lightning.

He accidentally obtains the tenderest result.
Still, you bide your time barely stirring your patience.

In the Nick of Time

You remember the evening you smoked with her
tipping your ashes into the same pink glass heart
already forgetting the recently steaming cabbage rolls
scooped like small fowl from the dark blue roaster
more speckled than any night sky,
you wondering whether her cigarette tasted of caraway
and she suddenly declaring the mimes you watched on PBS
were in league with the devil himself. Isn't everybody?

Now you think as you scour her apartment for valuables
which will mysteriously vanish during her final hospitalization.
The flippant remark intended to veer you away from argument
may be the reason your one living grandparent has not returned
to your house for dinner. You decide to take the silverware,
silently tarnishing in its velvet-lined mahogany chest,
the modest jumble of jeweled brooches in their gilt-edged box,
and the old Bible wrapped in tissue against the ravages of use.
You have been here in her absence only once before,
the last night you brought her home after dinner,
the same night you discovered too late the building was on fire
or at least filled with smoke and she had already seen
the lights whirling around her neighborhood and insisted
you investigate. Volunteers black-clad and fluorescently striped
moved through the hazy still glaring halls like confused mimes,
but her apartment was untouched. You spent three hours
in the hellish lobby with her wheezing her misery and worry
to her of the platinum wig and to him of the purple baseball hat,
to her of the dancing slippers and to him of the walnut cane,
to her of the aluminum walker and to him of the humped back.
You learned *angina emphysema insomnia osteoarthritis* and *ulcers*
the five vowels of old age your grandmother has patiently memorized
and will not survive. You have been to see her again.

~ Still Life ~

She still recognizes you even though you have denied her
please just one cigarette by feebly explaining the danger of oxygen.
When you leave her apartment, you will perform her quaint ritual
of departure the last time it will ever be performed.

THE POSSIBILITY OF TURNING TO SALT (1987)

Steel Mill Ornithology

As far as we know, here
no crane normally wades
among reeds in shallow water.
As far as we know,
there are just four species:
bridge, gantry, jib, and mobile,
all most commonly safety yellow,
all intelligent creatures,
able to dip, swivel, pivot, and glide,
while hoisting several times
their own considerable weight.
One subspecies of the mobile,
smaller and more agile,
is popularly called a *cherrypicker.*
Most cranes are extremely responsive
to humans.
As far as we know,
there is no such thing
as a whooping crane.

Man with Boots

Each sole is itself
larger than the man
relaxed behind them,
his legs foreshortened
to a denim bundle.
There is contrast
enmeshed in the fabric
and folded in the grainy leather,
as if subject mattered
less than texture. The man's shirt
is a plaid enlargement of warp and woof.

His fingertips touch—
a spider on a mirror—
as if he might be praying.

There is iced tea faintly glowing
in a striped glass so near his ear
he might be listening to it hum.
The coffee cup suggests presence
of someone wholly outside the picture.
The largest of three tomatoes
on the white railing shines.
There is backyard scenery
between the perfectly white balusters.

The man's speech halts
and stalls like traffic
as he tests his knuckles
against the ache he has achieved
in a tire shop. He knows his blood

is killing him. He may be pausing
en route to an elusive space.

He may be listening
to the sputtering engine of a small plane
in the sky beyond mingled sycamore
and tulip branches where
hawks glided earlier.
He may be listening for leaves.

He may be feeling the breeze
tickling his neck. He may be telling
his only secret—that he has no secret.

Or he may be recalling the earliest incident
he can remember: being in an olive room
with dressing women and their powdery smells
asking an innocent question regarding hair
and being escorted into dull yellow light
where men snickered.
His boots have new soles and heels.

Small Wonder

The sky has no color now
that the streetlights are on.
If I were twenty years younger,
the mercury vapor would be incandescent,
and I would have to be home by now

and probably sweating in bed
contending with starved mosquitoes,
but I'm on the back porch
watching robins come down to the yard
to feed, and the fireflies signaling,

one climbing the tulip tree,
a cat moving slowly across the yard,
and the robins dispersing.
I smell rain moments before
an extremely brief shower arrives.

The streetlights cast their shadows,
and the shadows gain definition.
A man I don't know,
wearing a pale green jacket,
walks by in the alley.

Moths gather at the streetlights
to commit their nightly error.
A breeze alters the elms slightly,
and robins stop calling.
Nothing will undoubtedly repeat itself.

The First Last Moon Poem
(To A Younger Brother)

Some days I swear to everyone
I have a brother in Korea
whose muscles buzz with high tension.
I tell them there's so much
raw electricity in your body
you glow at night in your bunk,
but no one here thinks
you're anything special.
Last night I watched the moon
through waves of heat rising
from a stack at the boiler house.
It was a lemon slice
sinking in some summer drink.
The funnels of smoke are still here
twisting from the black stacks
like oddly persistent tornadoes
or like dark bouquets
a good clean and strong wind
might scatter someday.
I stare at them sometimes
halfway expecting a crowd of genies
to materialize and start granting wishes:
trunks of jewels and gold coins,
the harems and limousines,
eternal youth, and stunning beauty,
the whole gleaming works
but nothing so far
not even a face.
Thanks for the gifts you sent
especially the jackets for Shane and Ivan.
Although they have trouble

with the left-handed zippers,
they're proud to have their names
embroidered on something they own.
An orange cat was dying this morning
in the safety between tire and curb.
As its poisoned belly shuddered
it nonchalantly licked itself
as if everything were taken care of,
the burial arrangements complete.
The shiny flakes of graphite
still fall continuously
but the stations announce
no measurable precipitation
in the past twenty-four hours.
I should've known
the kind of day it would be.
The boys watched a black
and yellow snake doing an odd dance
with a half-swallowed frog.
Shane finally answered his brother's
That frog was a bad frog, right?
with *It's okay Ivan. Frogs eat flies too.*
The whole thing seems important
but none of the neighbors will listen.
They go inside and take out
brochures describing retirement
communities in Arizona and South Carolina
where no children are allowed
and they reread and reread
as the light gets dimmer.
We're the richest city in the state now
highest per capita income
and the banks and credit unions
don't have deposit boxes available

because they're all stuffed
with coin collections
faces and dates unmarred unblemished.
So, all the wills and testaments
and paid-up policies
are rubber-banded and paper-clipped
and stored at home with color brochures
the edges and creases of all these documents
equally valued equally worn and frayed.
If you can help it
don't come home.
They'll get on your head
with talk of medical benefits
and the new regime at the mill.
They'll batter you with pleas
and warnings to forget paid holidays
but to press for better pensions
when the new contract comes up.
They'll tell you how sorry they are
for you because you're so young,
then ask you to have a look
at their cars or their televisions.
There's not a man left
in the valley who can fix
a leaky faucet or can lift
more than twenty-five pounds
without mechanical assistance.
If you can help it,
don't come home, because the moon
here is a clipped-off toenail
and you will always dream
of the places you left.

In Loco Citato

Deer still on the island venture
onto the slag perimeter road
to feed on corn thrown down
by the payloader operator.
The deer are not cunning.
This is simply the way it is
between them. I understand
this is not an experiment.
The spotlight of a tug
shoving barges upstream
sweeps the river
catches for an instant
a few deer on the island feeding
one or two of them looking up.
The light veers from bank-to-bank
but always returns to the herd,
as if whoever is at the light
doubts the deer exist.
The boat moves one way.
The river flows the other.
The deer continue feeding.
This is simply the way it is.
The operator knows deer
linger on the island.
He drops corn for them
or apples or whatever he has.
He sees the yellow deck-lights
of tugs on the river. At night
he loads conveyors with coke.
Although he works alone
building the huge coke piles,

he is not lonely. He sees
the beam sweeping back and forth
across the river. He sees it stop.

Deer still on the island venture
onto the slag perimeter road
to feed on ears of corn. Sometimes
truck drivers from the mainland plant
cross the bridge to the island
hoping to see a few deer.
A truck crosses the bridge,
moves along the idle battery,
past the quencher that never really worked,
past the empty and quiet payloader,
past the inclined conveyors.
The truck stops long enough
for a passenger to get out.
I have to bleed the propane
from a defective cylinder.
I walk over to the river.
A tire floats downstream.
The river is high and muddy.
I wonder how fresh the deer tracks are,
have barely enough time to look up
and see five or six deer stumbling
through the brush. Later
with propane still leaking,
I find corncobs on the slag road.

The Fifty Things Wrong with the Picture

None of this will hasten
or prevent that dazzling flash
astonishingly brief on the horizon.
Some of these children have never seen
a river or an orchard or a pea pod
before today. Poppies and impatiens
that make you think *cinnamon*
instead of *cinnabar* perhaps
are in simultaneous bloom
with tiger lilies and chicory
along the road and bachelor buttons
and clematis near the porch.
The children are without dread.
They investigate every crevice
for the golden apples they've heard
about. Only this morning
a man in khaki drove the green tractor
with its yellow wheels
through "that protected section, yonder"
beyond which coal is being stripped.
Two starlings chase a sparrow,
veering crazily but not dropping
the bread crust from its beak.
Not one detail here depends
on any other, not even the boy
in the chocolate and lemon polo shirt
about to discover a handful of bees.

Coincidence

Yes, I admit the sky
this morning was ominous:
those low-slung clouds
like charcoal smudges
dipping to efface the dunes.
And I too felt
as if we were being observed,
even as we noticed how languid
the gulls seemed as they fed,
and the dawning sun did pierce
the dreariness and shot
a beam right at us.
It was coincidence. Relax.
I doubt we'll end up holding hands
in somebody's watercolor
with a violent skyscape bleeding through it.
Things are not that way anymore.

Inertia

The law says nothing
about a body at rest
unwilling to remain so

yet unable to move. The radiant
orange slab slides from the furnace
settles into proper alignment

and glides toward the first mill stand.
The first ten or twenty
or even a hundred times you try

to anticipate the awful thud of
the sudden rooster tail
so you will not be surprised.

Once you've seen it, heard it,
felt it enough times,
you forget. The law

says nothing about the ability
of a body at rest, to simply absorb
the effect of an outside force

despite the overwhelming
inclination to move.

Stars and Stripes

Fun and Games were twin sisters
who set themselves on fire
to protest their mother's penchant
for turquoise furniture,
fuzzy slippers, and tangerine sundresses.
What finally set them off
besides the stolen sparklers
they jabbed at each other like insults
was the aqua and orange dinette suite.
They said the diagonal slashes hurt
their eyes and made life hideous.
Their mother claimed their flaming duet
was what was hideous and they were spiteful
witches. Fun and Games both recovered
enough to invest a fortune in mohair
sweaters their father could not resist
touching. They double-dated but did not marry
their high school's all-star backfield,
Cash and Carry,
who never amounted to much in football,
but distinguished themselves in business.
The twins did marry twins
Before and After
who would never consent to posing together
and went their separate ways.

In a Nutshell

Had you wanted apples
the mill would not be here.
This would still be orchard.

In Dubio

Smoke plumes coil in the valley
like cavalry dust, and irises
so purple they must ache bloom
in front of the white block wall,
but rescue is still improbable here
where the moon is as likely
to pass behind heated vapors
rising from a boiler house stack,
as if it were a lemon slice
sinking in some summer drink,
as it is to catch a locust branch,
delicate and vaguely Oriental,
lying across it like scrimshaw,
the same hour, the same night,
where cardinals nest in the wisteria,
Baltimore orioles in the sycamore,
and sparrows in the air conditioner,
where fresh asparagus is exotic
and men tend machinery all night,
as if it were troubled livestock.

In Embryo
"It's a good thing cats don't lay eggs."—P.K.

What I want is perfect orange
balanced between yellow and red,
neither yet both, like the seed
of bittersweet gathered in winter,
something related to cherry
and at least partly to blister,
to set in front of the window
where the hazy sun behind gauze
would accent the burst cases.
I sold handfuls to the woman
who once gave me a white shirt
for nothing, who fingered her buttons
nervously and lay it on the table,
carefully, as if it were fragile.
The orange I want is glowing
like the tubes in an old radio
maybe tuned to an historic Pittsburgh.
The announcer loves the Pirates.
You can mistake static for the crowd
noises, can almost smell the air,
imagine we're losing in the ninth,
maybe everything depends on Clemente
who may or may not make it to bat.
Or maybe it isn't old baseball,
but the tubes glow, and something stirs,
as if memory were caught in an updraft.
I am sitting in an oaken rocking chair,
one I bought from a widow
who made her living sewing.
For now everything here is quiet,
and I am thinking of an orange tea,

my body aching, twitching, and aging
while something besides tea brews.
If I only had the orange I want,
the solid, glowing orange of molten iron,
something like a toaster's grid,
Perhaps I could see the Chinese lanterns
again. It's a good thing cats
don't lay eggs; we might find them clustered
exactly where we least expected them,
say strung out along the baseboard.
They might be some shade of white
a delicate ivory, but with orange yolks.
I am daily getting old, but enjoy the plants
and lately think that if cats did lay eggs,
that would also be a good thing.
I wish you could see the silver maple sway.

In Absentia

Trudging up two hundred stairs
as if I knew what to expect
atop an idle blast furnace
I have come to see something.
This is what?
This is what I have?
This is what I have come to?
This is what I have come to see:

Ice particles streaming
out of swirling fog
form small white beards
on the yellow handrails.
I think of magnetism.
And there is nothing in the world
besides this small phenomenon
to notice—frost, not ice.
It happens often.
Last night near here
I saw a light behind louvers
and slowly twirling fan blades.
As far as I know
this could be a ship
on which I am alone.
I think of brevity.

In Propria Persona

Patches of locust bloom
like eczema or psoriasis,
whatever my father has on his elbows.
Beyond steeples and stoic roofs,
on the hill called Powerhouse
or Calico
lush clusters of white flowers
like those on black locusts
everywhere droop no more fragrantly
than they do anywhere
but those chumps signify
resurgence of forest
where ten years ago
not even grass grew.
The nightmares of falling
from the furnace into some ladle
of fiery slag soup
fade more each week I work
and once-barren hills
nurture new growth:
patches of locust trees.

In Excambio

Blue/orange flames arrive at dusk
to roost above the blast furnaces
north of town like large birds
flaunting their litmus plumage.
After I had sat awhile at midnight
with coffee on the back porch
trying to assess the drizzle,
lights at the Walnut Street junction
casting an amber glow on the mist
I realized the BOP looms
larger than most cathedrals.
The fiery birds flutter and preen
off and on like recurring dreams.
I went to sleep knowing summer
was going south for the winter,
even woke up cold once or twice
dreaming of rituals and worship,
priests wearing cobalt lenses
so they could peer into the vessel
and magical birds who vanish
against the pale sky at dawn.

In Alio Loco

In the next town south
(always another place)
there is a young woman
(young or not, always a woman)
who lives in a shed
(another place again).
Beneath the skylight
cut in the ceiling
she has placed a mirror
flat on her table
on which she examines
a ruby brooch,
as if it were a cluster
of red stars in the blue sky.
I will send a message
to her tonight. I will
walk down Purdy Lane
with a hand-shaped bottle
I've been keeping for this.
I will sneak behind
the yellow brick church
cross the parking lot again
asphalt glistening under mercury
vapor. I will follow
the outfield fence
toward the swirling willow
rising up beside the iron
railroad bridge.
I will find Harmon Creek
and drop my glass hand
into water that always flows
water that can not freeze

~ In Dubio ~

my glass hand holding
this message that will
somehow reach the young
woman living alone in her shed.
If you are the woman
I doubt you'd have me
which is not the point.
If you are the woman
who lives in a shed
I want to apologize
for blue/orange flames
atop the blast furnaces
and for the orange water
flowing in Harmon Creek
that can never freeze.

In Damno

I am still here.
The electric failed last night
when someone fleeing pursuit
crashed on Freedom Way
heading for the bridge.
I suppose suitable news
photographs have been developed.
There were sirens downtown
and people out with flashlights
as if searching for clues.
I went out to look at the mill
which has, as I suspected,
a separate power source.
I returned to my porch
smoked in the dark and thought
of lighting some kerosene lamps.
When the lights went out
I suppose the bridge itself
vanished. I am still here
afraid for now to move.

In Consideratione Praemissorum

Seven men sitting on a railroad tie,
ailanthus sprouting like tropical lies
against the blue corrugated sheet iron
behind them, lunch buckets and thermos bottles
open at their feet, all look up at once,
as if by plan. They seem dazed,
or astonished this could happen,
this one open, interminable second.
There is vacancy in their eyes.
They naturally think of home here
down home, down state, down "hoopy,"
where they return to hunt or just to touch
the leaves of a familiar bush
or to chase that old emptiness
or to cuss groundhogs or crows
in the corn and come back to tell it,
but right now, this instant,
they all know their break is over.

In Gross

This could happen anywhere
this smell in the air
like ozone and cordite,
this industrial musk
and this cup of coffee
steaming like a wound
or this sound of glass
like a whiskey bottle
spinning on asphalt,
this ticking sound
of beetles at the light,
all of it anywhere,
but this woman sitting
on this green glider
with paint flaking off,
this woman about to speak,
this woman only here.

In Rem Versum

One drink and I wanted to swing
from the hardwood Casablanca fan,
but Amos could not find the switch
so jingled some quarters and played
Sinatra on the dusty juke box
flashing chartreuse and violet.
Kimo snapped his fingers and laughed.
Lenore asked him to please leave
his clothes on this time which he did
until the song of celebration
got the best of him. Our steward
came in as plastic palms shimmied.
Another drink and I forgot time,
forgot Marxist implications
of what the press says we have done.
I knew I would go home and sleep.
I was okay when I went in
and asked my wife and her sad friend
to take a bubble bath with me.
Both women laughed when I snapped
my fingers and did my little dance.

In His Verbis

How the thunderstorm was a mad scenario,
and now, how the last orange petal on the poppy
registers a single tremor before it drops,
fluttering to the ground like the last sound
in a litany echoing in a massive hallway.
How there is failure in these words. And plague.
How there is panic and aftermath and warning.
How anything, humiliation, is possible, androgyny
or boredom. How I remember the graceful profile
on the cheap cameo pendant my mother wore.
How the cedar trees were monks coming in for vespers,
or soldiers, weary and silent, and how syrup
in the mouth is no longer sluggish.
How the mill is an animated jumble of hinges
and pipe, of cable, an overgrown amusement park,
without the lemonade, a chuckle got out of control.

In Medio

I don't notice missing fingers
anymore. I don't mention absence
at the knuckle. Details always vary
but there's no point in asking.
Gary smashed his ring finger
against a wall with a buster handle
for example then years later married
a Korean woman who divorced him.
You don't visit somebody's house and ask
why the phone doesn't ring. If only
my shadow had not once slid over her
in the grass beside a fountain
it might not have loomed on her wall.
I tell you I still see the guttering
candle on her dresser. I knew drifts
out back were shrinking in the rain.
It's tempting to say we need rain.
to feed rust or to suppress the smell
of creosote and we need to make steel
for rust to feed upon. It's tempting
to shrug and to leave it at that. Lying
perfectly still I heard tiny lightning
crackling in her hair as she flung
her sweater to the chair and danced
her jeans dance briefly against
the backlit flowered curtains. She
was a butterfly with stunted wings
when she unfastened her bra. I'm sorry
I know less now than I did then
but it can't be helped. You know
I get the feeling I'm being followed
by a silent but relentless glacier.

~ In Dubio ~

Sometimes I feel its breath on my neck.
Or I can hear grasshoppers flicking
their legs inside a three-pound coffee can.
I still remember how Robert sewed them together,
how long his grasshopper necklace kicked.
Look there. It's swinging upside down
to get at the mulberries only seven blocks
from our fully integrated steel mill.
Long live that male blue jay! Look,
that car wants to swallow the man
pouring water into its radiator.
I've been looking at myself. Somewhere
near here a woman sits with her cat.
She will soon wake up smelling odors
that worry her. I remember small leaves
like patches of brown skin pasted
to wet glass. I remember water seeping
into footprints. Just outside Cincinnati
I saw a pair of Cape buffalo mating.
I see mufflers strewn like torsos
along the highways. I know raccoons
and possums lick the salty asphalt
in spring. I saw sludge slopping
out of clam buckets. Now that I've slipped
over the edge I'm anxious.
Haven`t you noticed the change? I know
I should eat less and quit smoking.
I saw myself on a window. The man
asleep atop the made bed wore khaki pants.
He slept in the attitude of a prisoner
as if he were listening to faint murmuring
in the hollow of his elbow. I saw
a girl taunting her brother. Her hair
was a blonde flag her brother aimed at.

~ In Dubio ~

I believe he wanted to stone her to death.
I think the world is on fire. I saw
a sweatbees' nest—eight carcasses
oblivious to intrusion—and the one
living resident zipped at my wrist.
I sawed a four-by-four and exposed
white and nibbling larvae of some sort
suffering shock. I found a hollow pile
of feathers and bones where a pigeon
was dismantled by ants. It happens.
I must make arrangements I guess.
I've seen wondrous fish with gills sucking
thin air. I've seen wondrous birds
blown up like rags against the sky.
I've slept under a galvanized roof
ignoring hornets conferring in the rafters
while it rained. I've seen circular leaves
sprouted overnight in a tulip tree.
I collapsed in a blue wheelbarrow.
I've waited and waited and waited
at the windows of dead flies
in several dilapidated stations
my skeleton emerging at an increasing rate.
Treading water is not so simple.
I hope I see forsythia cascading again.
If I lose a foot or a finger in the mill,
if the roof collapses,
if nothing happens again or still,
if the mirror breaks,
if anything and/or whatever,
then so be it. Life's too short.

In Exitu

Dusk, mimosa leaves closing like pamphlets,
and the retarded boy wearing black boots
does not see the steps and falls on the low bank
he can not negotiate, and a yellow flash of oriole
streaks to the pine tree, and a jet leads its vapor trail
glowing against the gray sky, and a woman wearing an orange
scarf and a flowered dress stops to touch a fender,
and the retarded boy's father wheels a bike
down the steps, and the boy takes it by the handlebars
and walks beside it saying, "This is my hot rod," and pulls
the front wheel off the ground, and the bike clanks
when the wheel hits the sidewalk, and the boy takes his bike
around the block, and a robin ventures close enough
to me to inspect me one eye at a time, and flies away,
and the vapor trail slowly dissipates, and the oriole
has flown off somewhere, and the clematis is about to bloom,
not tonight, but maybe tomorrow, and the lady has managed
to disappear, and the yard ornaments designed to amuse
the retarded boy do not move, and the pine tree blends
into the background, and the mercury vapor flickers,
and the retarded boy is not back yet, and I worry,
and his porch light goes on, and the streetlight, too,
and I hear back-up alarms from the mill, and ore trains
being shunted at the junction, and I worry.

In Extremis

Coming here, I saw land billowing
as if a corner might flap up
and reveal massive gears perhaps
but there were cattle for ballast
and stitching disguised as fencing.
This is a place where light crashes
through spruce needles just outside
my window or crackles in cat fur.
Time seems to roll both ways at once
here. I saw a robin extract a worm
from one of its young then fly
backward to the ground where
it fed the worm to the earth
while the ice in my drink melted.
The language is familiar and deceptive.
A man said 'chair,' and the perfect chair
tumbled slowly through the air.
When I admired a woman breathing mauve
her breath faded to azure.
The odd music I heard this evening
was asphalt. The stone wall chants
a work song. I have chosen my epitaph.

In Adversa
(Some Fragments)

March is the nuthatch
skittering head-first
down the bare black walnut
or the bare silver maple.

April is forsythia
beneath hazy pastel willows
weeping over the bank
of the orange creek.

May is mock orange
scattered like mortar explosions,
the most delicate mist
rising all around.

June is the red squirrel
fleeing the blue jay
both of them caught in the morning
sun crackling in the sycamore.

August is sulfur
moths twirling above the crown
vetch, deer prints in silt
at the culvert.

September is crab
apples, so red
on the roadside
near the Tin Mill
carpenter shop.

October is a buck
swimming the river,
climbing the gray slag bank
toward red and yellow
trees on the island.

In Vadio

I will show you the oriole nest
it took me until March 11th to find.
I will show you the maimed sycamore
shriek of a tree that's endured
humiliation all along.
I will show you blue and orange flames
dancing instead of the moon
above the blast furnaces.
I will show you my glass hand
and introduce you to the woman
who lives in the shed with prisms
if I should recognize her.
I will show you garlic and rose of Sharon.
I will show you orange water
reflecting an iron bridge.
I will show you a lagoon.
I will show you the BOP* and the FPW*
although I can not take you inside either.
I will show you heaps of slag.
I will show it all to you.
I give you my word.

Mill divisions:
*BOP - Basic Oxygen Process
*FPW - Finishing Plant Warehouse

In Integrum

I've put a white shirt on
to celebrate my neighbor's roof,
the brick chimney leaning against its own shadow,
the nest of black branches above it all
dissolving into brilliance.
I've put my white shirt on
to celebrate cookies on a plate downstairs
and the pears and oranges in a bowl
with one perfectly curved banana.
I am celebrating the Christmas cactus
blooming in March.
I am celebrating nothing.
I am celebrating today.
I've put a white shirt on.

In Testimonium

It's hard to tell
whether drizzle here
is actually rain.
Both quenchers are idle,
but the scrubbers are not,
and steam traps hiss all night.
One day last week
cyclone fences
around the parking lots
were icy nets.
It's hard to tell
what's what here.
A salamander is a drum
of burning coke,
holes in it glowing orange.
One smoke stack is red and white
the others all black
or the color of liver.
Clouds are and are not clouds.
Rain is not always rain.

In Apertu Luce

The first plum blossoms
erupted today.
I could go crazy
and call the tree flotilla
while my son plays
"Santa Lucia" on his sax,
and my daughter claims
she sees strawberries
dangling in the sycamore,
and Raisin chases her tail
barking at the white tip,
but I stay on the glider
and tell Laurel again
about the cherry tree
as Shane starts
"The Marines' Hymn."

In Ambiguo

It is not my son practicing
scales on his saxophone,
notes rising from the cellar
to mix with mill noises.
Nor is it the tan dog
chained and going crazy
for the pair of sparrows
fluttering from the garage
to the still-bare elm.
Nor is it early constellations
of dandelions in the yard,
nor green paint
flcking off the glider.
It is not the cherry tree,
all beads and wire.
Nor is it the brown husks
fastened to the rose of Sharon.
It is something else.
It is not the oriole nest
glistening with cellophane
in the sycamore.

In Misericordia

The mimosa is sprouting now,
unfurling delicate fronds,
and there are wasps behind the shutter,
yet just two days ago,
a woman wearing a blue coat
slowly twirled
her beige umbrella in the rainy alley
before disappearing
beyond the lilacs blooming like an invasion.
Pollen, something in the fragrant wind,
has me weeping.

In Novus Ordo

The Mulkeys all have yo-yos
today, and they are casting
tiny planets here and there,
creating another universe,
ignoring the gray drizzle.
By this time next week
another gang of hoodlums
will again be gouging the shiniest cars
in the neighborhood
while the Baltimore oriole
fidgeting among the wet blossoms
in somebody's backyard cherry
ignores them. Maybe it will be
the 15th continuous day of rain.
For now, though, there is hope
sprouting between the bricks
in the Mulkeys' paved play yard,
and certainty springing from the hand
of every Mulkey child. Right now,
this minute, because some prodigal
Mulkey uncle has returned with gifts
for everyone, anything is possible.

In Iisdem Terminis

I'm on a clanking aluminum ladder,
calmly removing the green hysteria
we call shady wisteria
from the clogged downspout,
when a sparrow nestling flutters
up in my face, wings wild for escape,
landing at last on my chest, clinging
fiercely to my tee shirt, I cling
fiercely to the quaking ladder, and
nothing happens for a full second.
The bird stays attached to my chest
like a spare heart, terrified.
It finally lets go and glides
down to the maple, like a close call
shrinking in the rearview mirror.

In Re

The thing about this place, in the background,
wherever local scenery goes slack,
between houses snug as teeth, beyond trees,
the patch of corrugation or smoke stack,
the glimpsed steel coil or snatch of chain-link fence,
the flinty abundance of railroad track,
the thing all about this place, is the mill.
White petals of the black locust flutter
less like snow or ash than live confetti
to celebrate with summery clutter
some seasonal transaction otherwise
veiled from sight. And all we do is sputter
about increased turns on the platers, say,
knowing nothing of what happened today.

In Perpetuum

Say the word "when."
The mill sings it
this one word when
always, always
sustaining it,
without breathing
of course, one word
in monotone
an endless breath
neither joyous
nor in sorrow
but always, when.
It is the sound
of rpm's
in the millions.
when cicadas
wheezing/free us,
free us, free us,
get stuck on free,
think of the sound
of the word when.
What would happen
in its absence?
The sound remains
flawless, even
when masked by rain.
What would happen?

In Arbitrium Alieno

The porch is different
from every other,
including the one
it was only yesterday.
Someone has hung
a squid-shaped ornament—
rainbow-colored drum and streamers—
next to the plastic white thermometer
displaying Fahrenheit and Celsius.
Six brass horses
dangling from the omega
of a thin house shoe
prance against each other.
No bird in its right mind
would take up residence
in the raw clay birdhouse
barely the size of a human heart
or a coffee mug,
but ruby-throats have been known
to visit the tubular feeder.
Even now, this porch is different
than it was a minute ago.
The glider's green paint is flaking off.
The geranium trembles in the breeze.
A wasp arrives in the rafters.

In Banco

Beneath two hawks exploring thermal plumes
Of lacquer-laced exhaust, the bench is spread:
Industrial peninsula that fumes
With thinner vapors. Deer, of course, have fled.
And in the storage shed, a man dozes,
Ignoring hornets. As sweat trickles down
His cheek, he dreams of galvanized roses
Against his will, in self-defense, a frown,
And how the river freezes in winter.
He lithographs beer labels on tin sheets,
But not by choice. His dreams, he feels, splinter,
Yet little naps remain his sweetest treats.
He knows about the hawks, the deer, and guilt,
But can not say how his future was built.

In Medias Res

The ailanthus I found
thriving amid strewn junk
in the abandoned Open Hearth
should not have surprised me,
yet it was somehow lovely
among the cracked trunnions
as it aspired to the latticework
of trusses supporting nothing but sky.
Growing as it did on a steel slab
with nothing beneath but basement,
it was vital yet doomed, and still
an ordinary tree of heaven.

In Personam

Mercury vapor drifts through the bedroom
screen along with the mill's concerted whine,
that monotonous lullaby. I lie
awake listening to engines shunting
gondolas at the Walnut Street junction
and thinking the maple leaves must tremble
with the racket glancing off them like light.
Who is at fault for my insomnia?
It is not the man who founded the mill,
nor the engineers and brakemen who let
the cars slam tonight, nor whoever lights
this city with vaporized mercury.
I put my body to this noisy test,
use it at the mill, now wish it would rest.

In Actu

Looking back now, I arranged everything:
thirty tracks glinting in the amber light
shed by three high-voltage clusters
perching brightly atop their standards
to illuminate the empty rail yard,
and the fringe of forest slipping down
the hill. I knew black bricks formed
jagged black letters on the stack
above the unused incinerator
like separate faces on a totem.
The name of the town had to be there.
The lagoon had to be there behind
the silhouette of bunched trees rising
to escort Harmon Creek away from
the lumber company buildings painted orange,
past the ball field and its dugouts
behind Kroger's and the Ford dealership.
It was night, and streetlights
had to be strung out like constellations
in all the declining neighborhoods.
Two plumes rose and merged
above the hydrochloric acid plant,
and traffic thumped across the Lee
Avenue railroad bridge, headlight beams
briefly flashing up to escape the planet
before the jolt yanked them back.
The long low buildings, of course,
had to be there, black even in daylight,
lying south to north as if magnetically
aligned. I live beyond them.
I know there is a powerhouse above me now
squatting like a duck on the brow of this hill.

In Notus

Toward the end, neon gave way
to clusters of fluorescence on the horizon,
like shimmering oases,
or notes of a difficult melody.
Birds fled the sanctuary,
graffiti appeared on the footbridge,
and sprouting vines strangled the pines
while shingles blew off the shelter roof.
He wrote toward the end: "I fear death
may be nothing but acute nostalgia,
so continue my maintenance dose
of the daily world for now,"
how burst paint blisters in the mill
trap graphite as if it were precious,
how Delbert said he heard whales
mating outside the locker room,
meaning some alarm sounded like their whistles,
and how I listened hard
but heard only steam escaping,
and thought of "spuming."

In Continenti

You've been fixing the car in the rain
outsmarting the old parts and rust again,
but lying on wet asphalt this time
installing a new muffler against the noise,
maneuvering the new tailpipe over the axle,
clamping them together for the sake of exhaust.
You've been fixing the loose door handle.
You've been wiping your hands on a rag.
You've been fixing the heater.
You've had your head up under the dash.
Your back is killing you again.
How can you think of writing a poem
while you soak in the hot water
barely touching your fingertips together
deciding what it must be you feel?

In Ipsis Faucibus
for J. M.

What he did that night
at the mill gate was his own
way of saying goodbye:
he danced the hoochie koochie:
put his left foot in
(as if testing water),
took his left foot out,
put his right foot in,
(as if deciding how to begin),
took his right foot out.
(Plant Security gathered all about.)
The problem was he didn't know
which was in and which was out
whether he was coming or going,
so to speak. He'd lost touch
and didn't know whether the mill
was real or the town was real
(like a dreamer dreaming he's dreaming).
This happened at gate one.
Almost everybody thought
he'd taken too many pills,
but that wasn't it.
Have you ever been through a mill gate?

In Multum

The white dog sleeping on the roof
of the white car sunk to its frame
in front of the peeling yellow house
could be a sign of things to come.
The river was olive drab today
despite glaring sunlight, the window
pane old enough to have character.
The rusting flag pole wavered.
Later, a spaniel sitting patiently
in the driver's seat of a Bronco,
like somebody's sad, brow-beaten mate
stunned with the unfairness of it all,
whatever it all might ever be,
who might have been fantasizing
murder or contemplating money problems
or suicide or even simple flight,
observed me through the steering wheel,
and I thought about imperfections
in the glass, how they are always perfect
no matter what effect they have.
Later still, the white dog barked
from the pinnacle of his empire,
claw marks on the dull finish,
dried splashes of slobber
on the smudged and murky windows,
the heavy collar around his neck hooked.

In Rerum Natura
for J. S.

The single falling monarch
wing—the tiger flake—
fluttered down outside
the blast furnace locker room
turning over and over
like a leaf or litter
exploring a diagonal
so close to me
it might have drifted
all the way through me.
I'm not so sure it missed.

In Tenebris

Here the soul acts like a lozenge.
Imagine a man peeling off
Many layers of clothing: his blue woolen coat,
His drab field jacket, his checkerboard wool shirt,
His plaid flannel shirt, his quilted thermal underwear,
His cotton tee shirt. His body,
Black hairs sprouting in the usual patterns,
Is not the heart of the human onion.
Nor is his heart, not here.
Imagine him unzipping his skin, shedding it,
Snapping his rib cage apart, and finally
Unsnapping his heart.
That pitted lozenge is his soul.
That shrinking pitted lozenge
He's been protecting all these years,
Trying to keep it warm,
So the insect inside it
Like a prototype mosquito
Trapped in amber will live.
That pit, his soul,
One fine day will disappear.

In Cardine

It was mild for any January morning,
over forty and drizzly
from the turn-around
at the end of Elm Street,
I saw three deer
browsing at midfield
in Jimmy Carey Stadium.
From time to time, one looked up
as if it expected disturbance.
Three bright lights jiggled
under the bridge crane
above the scrap pile
beyond the northern end zone.
The black corrugated hulk
that is the Sheet Mill
loomed above the visitors' bleachers.
A man came out of the carpenters' Quonset hut
beyond the dressing room and spat.
The most fidgety doe looked up
and bent back to the grass.
Something shifted—
perhaps the hillside woods
behind the press box
slipping imperceptibly closer.

In Dorso

Light. Sparkling graphite particles
pour through the broken window
like millions of wild ions.
The man lying on one of the benches
in the laborer's shanty has a world
attached to his back for now
depending on how you imagine him,
yet he is not a mythical figure.
He lies with his eyes
closed in the hollow of his elbow
and remembers a rabbit looking at him
or a sparrow landing on a brazier
and regarding him with one eye,
then the other, then flying away.
How is it his body is at rest
while he has a world on his back?
He lives in a house with one
functional chimney that ascends
in a plaster shell through his bedroom
functioning as a pilaster,
something to hold the wall up.

In Bonis Defuncti

Sewn behind the circular patch
embroidered SPACE FOR RENT
on the brow of his yellow golf cap
this message folded inside
a paper crane:

If what I have written
in my own hand
had been origami
it would have been considered
lovely and miraculous:

the blue/orange flames
roosting at night
instead of the moon
above the blast furnaces,
like birds with litmus plumage,
miraculous and lovely.

In Aegri Somnia

This heat makes it
almost impossible to sleep,
but easy to say the blast furnaces
north of town make me think
saguaro. Sometimes
I think I'd rather live
in some more temperate zone,
amid less brutal scenery,
where people are familiar
with public fountains, say,
or jazz at noon saturating
the plaza, small round leaves
quivering in the ornamental trees,
but I know this is weakness.
It is this life that makes
another life possible.
Blast furnaces actually resemble
the great muscles they are,
huge pipes curving around them
like venae cavae, like aortae.
If it takes a desperate mind
to imagine they resemble saguaros,
then I guess mine is.

In Bono et Malo

Except for two dogs,
and the children lolling
about in sleeping bags
in the coolest room upstairs,

we are alone for once
early Saturday morning.
I'm eating toast, and
I crave strawberries.

When I mention this,
she lowers the straps
of her orange nightgown,
and smiles, wickedly.

In Folio

One thing at a time: the blue garage
is set so far into the alley's embankment
its gable roof is an easy step up.
Seven children lie on the gray shingles
like supine corpses in fierce sunlight,
unnaturally still, one still clutching
a stick, another a toy automatic.
It is some kind of drill, I guess,
because they all move at once, as if on cue,
and scramble yelling up to the ridge,
and one by one jump to the other side.
It's hard to believe any one of them,
perhaps the blonde with the stick,
could someday foster a tumor
growing like a hive in the rafters,
a tumor that might slowly crack a rib,
like in Delbert's first wife, so young.

In Simili Materia

When she stopped on the sidewalk
near the yellow storm drain,
near gnats swarming above the hedge,
the little girl perhaps three,
yelled something unintelligible
at the doll in the pink carriage.
When she slapped her baby
I remember flocks of pigeons
erupting from beams and ledges
at the Sinter Plant,
how they would flutter and circle,
flickering in the sun, and always
return to their niches to roost.

In Plano

Because hills are not on the maps
it's easy to get lost here; distant
neighborhoods appear to be adjacent.
A woman asked me today
how to get to Gate #1
and suddenly I was lost:
Why would anybody
who does not know
where Gate #1 is
want to get there?
The mill of course
is not on the maps.
So, I imagined the photograph
my friend said his mother had
of a man and a woman
at the Half Moon farm
site of the mill's FPW—
twenty-four acres under one roof.
The photograph was taken
after a flood (1936?)
and the man was proud
of the catfish he had caught
in the muck with his pitchfork.
It was as tall as he was.
For a time, I could no more tell
a woman how to get to Gate #1,
though I was headed there myself
than that catfish could have told
what year it was or what FPW would mean.

In Esse

Houses neat as teeth
run along an opposite ridge
toward a red brick powerhouse.
At sundown they are weird

birds glancing here and there
as they follow their mother
her plumage changing through violet
through purple on its way to indigo.

I saw her struck once
by lurid green lightning
but she absorbed the jolt
swallowed it as it were

easily as a duck would bread.
It was something to see.

In Posse

We collect postcards here
from unfamiliar regions
and examine them with some reverence.

We like to think for example
there is a bear somewhere
knee-deep in pure surge and froth
slapping salmon to a pebbly bank,
aspen twittering in the background
about the impending feast
under the glossy cobalt sky.

We like to think our bridge transcends
its obvious utility,
that its details are significant,
the powdery effect of primer
showing through faded aluminum paint,
the frayed cable ends,
the guardrails nicked and gouged,
the grating deck that hums and clanks.

If we were not so busy here
we might travel farther and more often.

In Absurdo

An old kitchen faucet hangs
on a clothes-line hook
screwed into the blue garage,
its thin supply-tubes crimped

like the copper legs
of some chrome bird.
It is not a trophy,
and the paint is blistering.

A can of "federal blue" enamel
dangles in the grimy window,
and a plastic ball floats in the catalpa
like a lost blue planet.

In front, two peonies,
one white, one red,
bloom like a political argument,
each its own perfect example.

In Ipissima Verba

I could never explain
how the word *array*
describes the principle
of frond arrangement
in black walnut trees
to anyone in the mill.
Forget the black locusts
erupting here and there
across the strip-mined fields
like mortar explosions.
I'm still working on the swirl
of all the weeping willows.

No. You go through the gate
and no matter what time it is
you say, "Morning," all day long
knowing maybe you're the only one
who knows you're in mourning,
and you call everybody "Uncle,"
and everybody in the mill
has the same middle initial,
which doesn't stand for Francis,
and you tell Uncle Melanie
F. Risovich you love her
and want her to have your babies
so she'll know you're crazy,
and tell Uncle Stephen F. Christian
you love him and want him
to have your babies so all of them
will already know you're crazy
in case you ever find yourself
for no apparent reason

so unaccountably joyful
you start yammering
about how birds feed or fly
or various aspects of design
you see in different trees
or how you feel like the young girl
you once saw doing one-handed cartwheels
down the middle of Elm Street
her blonde hair sweeping the asphalt.

In Praesentia

The others have left me behind
and taken an excursion to the backcountry
where in-laws are thick as thieves,
so I am here appreciating thirteen trees
in the yard: black scavenger ants
crawling the Norway maple like relatives
waiting for probate, the mimosa's leaves
collapsing every night like tiny governments,
the black walnut and the silver maple
tolerating one another like ordinary neighbors,
three mulberries beneath the tulip
like fruit-stands in the oppressive shade
of a bank building, the American sycamore
shedding leaves and sheets of bark-like rags,
the cherry and two wormy plums biding time
like social security recipients, and the rose
of Sharon littering the lawn with torpedo-shaped
blossoms which the ruby-necks have abandoned.
I've found a pastel portrait my mother did
of me when I was a young boy. God.

In Otium

What you do here for entertainment is
you visit the bus station early
to get the Wheeling paper and to see
the latest Little Egypt dressed,
dressed for breakfast, dressed for travel.
She wears favorite cowboy boots,
and you stare at the sky-blue leather,
the stitching around the stars.
Last night, it was impossible to think
she could be somebody's wife,
somebody's daughter, but today she is,
and her husband is sullen, or surly.

You check the reliable smokestacks
above the hydrochloric-acid plant.
Anyone in town can forecast
what little weather you have.
Picnic tables remind you
of lunchrooms in the mill.
If you don't get up and take a walk
you will go to sleep on the bench,
where ants will explore the fabulous terrain,
calculating how to carry you off.

At night your porch is bathed
in the purple glow of a bug fryer.
With the radio tuned to the Pirates,
you have another beer.

You have no use for dactyls or iambics.
You visit your sick and bury your dead.

In Periculum

The calliope puffs out clots of steam
behind the marvelous Delta Queen,
"The Beer Barrel Polka" echoing across the river,
white splotches hanging briefly in the air.

before dissipating like ordinary music,
the paddle wheel slapping and thrashing
water, the wake spreading across the olive surface,
small waves eventually washing over rubble

along both shores. Brightly colored automobiles
of Sunday drivers flit behind the trees
on one bank, and goldfinches flit
through ailanthus on the other.

The delighted passengers gathered around
the shell contraption, their pastel clothes
shining in sunlight, sing and clap
as the boat thumps its way downstream,

but the boat will barely clear the arching bridge
linking Brown's Island to the east bank.
The passengers on their perilous journey
enjoy themselves, each other, privilege.

Any minute, though, something might rupture.

In Deceptio Visus

By now, the clapboard siding
on the other side
of this linen-textured wall
is no longer barn-red.
It is maroon in the failing light,
becoming purple. An hour ago
we saw ourselves in this window
pausing to notice where we were
at the time, on the sidewalk,
yet superimposed on the window,
a used-car lot blooming behind us,
thin Venetian blinds, open,
behind the glass, this spider plant,
hanging behind the blinds,
and presumably, the rest of the room
behind the plant, but really,
just a sense of depth
we thought must be a room.
Now we have moved inside,
and the used cars are over there,
across the street where they belong,
for now, and we are here,
at this table, with coffee,
the surface of mine giving off vapors
we assume are coffee,
and wobbling gently
with some minute movement
of the universe which is otherwise
undetectable, except
for the spider plant shimmering
slightly, which lets us know

the building itself is shaking.
When did you first notice
the goldfish swimming
in the lighted tank across the room?

I want to tell you it could be
heavy traffic somewhere nearby
slowly shaking the whole town down.
It could be the steel mill,
which is the reason for the traffic.
Had we examined our reflection
more closely, we might have seen
that plume of smoke, there, curling toward us.

In Linea Recta
"Rattle of contents is acceptable in this type of merchandise."

1959 was a pivotal year
for Ruth and Charlie.*
They already had four boys,
and though they didn't know it yet,
Ruth was finally pregnant with Theresa.
Charlie had a new job,
a promotion, from the mill
to the old General Office.
In December, they bought a new house
two miles away. They loaded
their new, aqua-and-white station-wagon,
made fifty trips up two hills,
their furniture always in danger
of sliding out.
         How was I to know,
riding on that green tailgate,
a purple dresser wanting to push
me to the blurred asphalt
running away from my feet,
that in a quarter of a century,
I would be sitting at a window
remembering that warm December day
when I was eight years old
and trying to understand what happened,
how that practically innocent boy
came to inherit a steel mill
thumping in his chest like a heart attack?

*Ruth and Charlie…Tim Russell's parents

In Loco

The aluminum girl on the lawn
will not look up from her aluminum book
to admire pink windows at dawn.
She ignores weather, traffic splashing by,
pedestrians, even the bronze night sky
flashing with industrial fire.
She has never seen the oak tree
full of brown and curled leaves like birds
that always seem ready to flee.
She wears a blouse without sleeves
and a peasant skirt. She is barefoot
because it will always be summer.
She has never turned a page
and has no idea she's a statue.

In Haec Verba

Red and white midgets practice
formations and blocking assignments
in the outfield. There are railroad cars
beyond the fence—some SOUTHERN boxes
filled with kitchen cabinets
on the lumber company siding
three anonymous black tankers
on the black iron bridge with the silvery
green willow swirling up behind it
like an all-purpose prayer.
A CHESSIE SYSTEM black cat looks on.
There is a necklace of maroon CR hoppers
almost bulging with ore pellets
about the color of dried blood
strung along the bottom of the hill
presiding over the entire scene
like a judge passing sentence.
There is withered chicory in the wire.

In Deliciis

When Violet spells **laundry**
I hope she never hears it
used in a sentence
the way my mother did.

I daydream, smelling **watermelon,**
noticing the lighted clock,
but the time itself is lost.
We are all here in limbo, waiting.

When Ivan spells **barricade**
I think he already knows
something will come between us
in a few short years.

At the end of every round
there is polite applause
masking the sound of **exodus**
thudding its murmuring rumor
across the gymnasium floor.

Clusters of siblings and parents
in the **amber** varnished bleachers
thin out like vegetation
at the edge of an advancing desert:
time-lapse photography.

Words fly like those indoor
airplanes old men design
solely to prolong slow-motion flight
beneath an **ornate,** vaulted dome,
but Violet, in corduroy, brings me back

with **stagecoach,** and I think
about old movie heroes
I hear the word **scarecrow**
and imagine one shouldering a large bird
like a pirate with his parrot.

When Ivan spells **chimpanzee,**
six of the fittest still survive,
half a dozen children remaining
to cast their spells on the judges.
There is a lull in the competition.

Violet is first in line at the microphone.
She frets, having never heard
the word **deacon** before,
and moments later when Ivan stalls
on the word **escalator**

I mutter my own word: **incarcerate**
which has fluttered around me
like a monarch these twenty years
always just out of reach
waiting for the right moment to land,

and **prophetic.**

In Adversum

For forty-five minutes I told
my foreman lies about my brother
Wallace—how after half a lifetime
of trying, Wally finally managed
to get himself struck by lightning
on a sunny day, like a poet,
and how Wally dropped everything
climbed into his old green Buick
and headed downstate to find
a thirty-foot walnut log, how
blue exhaust twirled behind him
like a tornado lying down on the job,
and how he brought the log back
and how he uploaded it in his yard,
and how he carved his totem
although he'd never done much
of anything with tools before,
and how he got me and half
his neighborhood to struggle with it,
like ants with a grasshopper leg,
until his wife finally took over
and we got the thing planted for him—
for forty-five minutes I went on,
holding the Bogeyman Frank at bay
while I was supposed to be painting
a cage, a wire-mesh cage. I was proud
because he asked me if it was true.
"It would be," I said,
"if I had a brother named Wallace."
"Paint the damned cage," he said.

In Diem

Although it is warm for October
seventh, his field jacket
(olive drab) (and paint-speckled),
is slung over his shoulder because
there was frost this morning

and thick fog near the river.
Greeting his wife in their garden
he sets his black lunchbox down
among fallen silver maple leaves.
She has a colander filled with broccoli.

One of their children comes to help
gather the last of the black walnuts,
searching two clumps of pale peonies
for the mottled green pods.
There is Swiss chard and one tomato.

The man follows the woman and the boy
to the house, stooping for a leaf rake
he leaves at the door, where he turns
out of habit to check the sky,
a few white clouds sailing overhead.

In Vivo

Tonight, I briefly thought I might explode
In blossom: Once it startled me to think
My blood could circulate a lethal code
Or I could somehow die without a wink
To signal quick return, but now I know
How tenuous my hold is on this life.
(You think you know the scarlet river's flow
Requires its secrecy, you love your wife.)
Until a cure is found for my disease—
So many cases I cannot say it—
Some simple scum, say, derived from peas,
Enough pain accepted will delay it.
Let blood sustain its damaging rumor;
Let me maintain this droll sense of humor.

In Judicio

I admit I saw the woman
that night across Main Street
from the creche (four shepherds.
some sheep—one black—
three kings, two camels—
one saddled with a pack,
so obviously one missing—
an angel wired awry,
a mule, a cow, some straw,
and that nuclear family).
There were white rags
tied to wires like upside down doves.
This woman had an umbrella
but it was not raining.
Behind the stable scene
there were soggy flowers
in front of the purple granite memorial.
A squad car stopped traffic
while an ambulance started
for the nearest hospital.
A streetlight flickered out,
then flickered back on.
I spoke to the woman,
and she to me about weather.
She closed her umbrella.
When she left, she said something
about "flu weather" and "nut rolls."
I stopped in the library
for an address, which I got,
and Fatima accused me of quiet
when I left a few minutes later.
I did not go straight home.

I saw bare light bulbs
through flimsy bedroom curtains.
I saw two white wreaths made of plastic
sandwich bags. I found
a dark blue hat with a yellow logo
on the pavement. It was drenched
and gritty. I hung it
on somebody's chain-link fence.
It was the night of the Gemini
meteor showers. But there were clouds.
It was too warm for snow,
too warm to smell coal smoke.
As I left the library,
I saw the aluminum girl
reclining on the lawn,
and her tree still full of brown leaves.
There was some activity
beside the fire department,
pine trees for sale, I think.
One of the doors—the left one—
had a decorated tree painted on it.
The station was lit up,
but I did not go there.
I did not see the woman again.
She was not wearing such dark lipstick
that night. I saw a coffee pot
being put in a window
above Sunday's sermon's topic:
ANGELS. I had to squint to read it.
I remembered Poyner's poem, "The Acolyte,"
which has angels in it transformed into animals.
More traffic splashed by.
I carried a green notebook.
I guess I am guilty of something.

In Transitu

Feverish or not, I wake up thinking
the green dial is a luminous city
floating beneath its stereo-light moon,
a tenuous indication of strength at best.
This is flu season. The rainy piano
has stopped for technical reasons, yet
my set receives the silent broadcast.
Outside in the yard, the palimpsest
of trampled snow slowly disintegrates,
holes in it growing like some virus.
I have reached for the toggle
that will banish this city in crisis
when two flutes tentatively begin.

In Locus Delicti

Frozen grass crunched underfoot.
The polar breeze was important:

a thousand plastic grocery bags
filled with air and possibility

drifted through the neighborhood,
rolling gently and bouncing

across the streets and yards,
cellophane tumbleweeds humping along

toward the next country.
Bare hedges snagged a few.

Others roosted in the lower branches
of ornamental trees, like fruit

some wonderful winter fruit.
Or they might have been a virus.

So much depends on state of mind.

In Aequo Animo

Later, when it's over,
when you are waiting
for the light to change
at the Market Street Bridge,
although it defies reason
to wait at two in the morning
on this deserted stretch,
after your sleep
has been interrupted
by the telephone
and you have answered
your mother's summons
and driven through snow
to your childhood home,
after you have crept
down squeaking stairs
into the gray cellar
you still think of as yours,
and showed your own father
how to relight the furnace pilot
and you have come back up,
and had a cup of coffee,
while you waited with your mother
for the house to warm up,
later, when either way,
you are halfway home,
and a red traffic light
in the middle of nowhere
vanishes, and the green
suddenly appears,
you calmly understand
this was a dry run.

Jade Plant

Some days I think it must be a green chorus of voices
joined in a silent medley of anguish you can almost see.
Every week there's more. Or is it somehow rejoicing?

Some days the plant is an ideal audience, or sentry,
listening in all directions for the smallest hint of truth,
or relief. I know it suffers more than a little

too much water sometimes, not enough at others,
but the brown scaly patches are symptomatic of nothing
more than maturity. Despite the uncertainty,

another pair of pale and shiny ears, or mouths
has sprouted lately. Some days the plant is a gossip,
some days, an arthritic penitent with nothing to confess

but swollen with the need for discussing it anyway.
Some days this guardian at the window
whispering instructions to itself just waits,

succulent and tender as the idea of an undeclared lover.

Theory and Practice

She laughs like water
twirling out of the sprinkler,
splashing the azalea,
the lopsided rhododendron,
and the top-heavy clematis,
but drenching the parched grass.
She laughs like water
whether I need it or not.
Sun glistens in the drops.
She laughs at all my wild promises.

A Portrait of Frank & Kevin as a Pair of Yard Flamingos

They are both relatively bright,
even brilliant in certain light,
and radiant, as if lit from within.

Today they are grazing on plantain
beneath the struggling mulberry,
Frank whispering what sounds like Latin

but could be surreptitious advice
to the lovelorn, and Kevin pretending
he doesn't hear. Frank wants Kevin

to stop nibbling and notice the stupid
robin perched atop the rusty flagpole,
but Kevin will not oblige.

Kevin wants Frank only
to admire his elegant neck.
Although he has one just like it,

Frank cannot resist. He is quiet
for a minute, but then resumes chattering
about the self-important robin,

the olive river, wisteria tendrils
high in the ailanthus, the murderous
tenacity of whiskey weed,

a fantasy round of golf
with a penguin named Mario,
and a new theory of camouflage.

Kevin will not lift his head,
even when two biplanes come over the hill,
because he knows he will weep.

The Ugliest Flower in the World

I slept on my arm,
leaving the red imprint
of my own ear on the biceps,
as if an arm could hear things,
or listen, a flower so ugly
it hurt. My arm was crippled
with the news surging inside it,
or was it only rumor? I wanted
to kiss that ear,
to whisper some sweet nothing.

Pigeon

Thirteen shades of gray,
including dove, including pearl,

an iridescent neck,
orange claws, orange beak,

obsidian eye
more than the sum of your parts

stoic on your filthy pedestal
at the end of the Open Hearth,

like some dim-witted sentry,
posted to be seen,

your belly full of corn
laced with hallucinogens.

Quit looking at me.
Don't you know it's quitting time?

Honey Locust

Despite the torture
of repeated amputation,
the sycamores here are lovely.
The single elm, of course, is doomed.
Insinuated amid the others
corralled on three sides
by galvanized guardrails,
a honey locust rises
like a primitive arsenal
above the scarred table
and the concrete planter
stuffed with geraniums,
so red you wonder if
they cry out at night.
Thousands of tiny swords
fastened to the trunk
and many more hidden in the leaves
threaten the children
who venture in to swing
higher and always higher,
toward what little sky there is,
or merely dig in the dirt,
with traffic swishing past,
a muffler gurgling now and then.
Some of the children
have called the thorns "warheads"
yet they know no dread.

For All I Know

I have imagined her among tiger lilies
beyond a low stone wall painted white.
I have imagined her lurking at dusk
beneath the barren mulberry; or stooping
for a blue fragment of a robin's eggshell,
the robin somewhere nearby asking,
"Where do you eat?" twice every five seconds.
I have imagined her masturbating in a catalpa,
arching her back but never quite crying out,
looking up through the leaves, astonished
to find the sky so milky, but not crying out.
I have imagined her prowling the neighborhood.
I have imagined her parked at the Riverside
Methodist Church, waiting for something to happen.
I have imagined her crimping her hair.
I have imagined her luscious bush.
I have imagined her practicing her loose-hipped stroll
in the cemetery, placing a found bird nest
on the stone of some perfect stranger.
I have imagined her memorizing names and epitaphs.
I have imagined her sitting in a basement
tavern, observing the rack and ruin.
I have imagined her holding a clump of blue
chicory, looking at it through inexplicable tears.
For all I know, I have imagined her.
For all I know, she is nothing but synapse.
For all I know, I do not love her.
For all I know, she never meant to seduce me.
I have imagined her.
I have imagined her dancing naked,
twirling her hands above her head
before a mirror with black flaws in it.

Nothing More, Nothing Less

I am out here in the fog
before the sun comes up,
watching the river glide,
taking a while to decide
if the river is not, in fact,
flowing, or slipping past,
or sliding, but gliding,
slow and unwrinkled
beneath the fog it's been
giving up all night.

I am out here in the fog,
scared to death of dying
inadvertently, by my own hand,
listening to a shrill jay
and invisible mill traffic
speeding on the river road.
Slowly twirling eddies of mist
rise from the warm, or cool,
I cannot decide which, dark
olive, seductive river.

I am out here in the fog.
I am out here waiting.

What We Don't Know Hurts

This could be ground zero:
a trucker in his sleeper at the Half Moon
marshalling yard, one hand at his crotch,
the other flung above his head
as if he were dreaming rodeo,
his snakeskin boots standing on the seat
as if riding shotgun for the night.
The man twitches, and maybe that is all.
Earlier, he stood with two others
and listened to the story about
"that old boy who put a cruiser
greasy side up in the grass
without even blinking his eyes.
Didn't see nothing, didn't hear nothing,
didn't feel nothing, and didn't blink.
Yessir. Ain't a speck of doubt in my mind.
That old boy was on autopilot."
But those two are long gone now,
each hauling twenty tons of steel somewhere,
and this one wakes up having to piss.
In a minute, he is wandering
across the practically deserted pavement,
and maybe that is all. In another part of town,
timed spotlights go out, and the pure
white spindle holding night off
the Methodist church vanishes.
In yet another part of town,
a young woman who has swallowed her tongue,
disappears beneath a manhole cover.
None of her three most recent lovers
noticed she was in trouble
until it was too late, so they leave her

where the next thunderstorm,
if there ever is one, will find her,
half a mile from the new hospital.
One lights a cigarette before he reaches
for the car door, and maybe that is all.

Don't Get Up

Another overloaded train
drags itself, screeching
and moaning through town
as if pain could build
character after all.
Some of the maroon cars
have messages scrawled on them,
but we've seen them all before
and don't get up.
Tangled in our bedclothes,
we embrace each other,
waiting for the blasts
before the last crossing,
and it's over before we know it.

The Motor

Now that we have failed,
now that I have snipped five tin circles
from the flattened tomato can
and notched them into fat *aitches*,
now that you have taped them together,
winding the wrong sized wire around them
to form your homemade armature,
now that the concrete Presbyterian belfry
has chimed "Amazing Grace,"
and I have shown you how
the sycamore's seed pods are bursting,
showering their white contents
diagonally through the bare tulip tree,
now that I have taken the risk
of slicing my thumb instead of yours,
and I have told you the name I had
for sycamores when I was your age,
namely "monkey-ball trees,"
now that I have sworn you to secrecy
and ruined the shape of the electromagnet
so badly the motor will never work,
now that I have done something for you
my father never did for me,
now that I have convinced you of our failure,
will you remember this evening,
how purple spikes of the peonies
here at the head of the garden
poke through the clump of daffodils?
Will you say a few kind words
over my dead body someday?

The Mechanic

Before his ruined fingers
even find the latch
he already has an idea
about what is wrong.
He has listened
and will not be surprised
when the hood rises.
He has seen every state
an engine can be in.
At night he has seen
tiny blue lightning
snapping around like
neural messages in a brain.
He can dismantle an engine
and reassemble it
without destroying it,
something no poet can do.
He knows about the hot sex
of pistons and cylinders,
how they fit together.
He knows no engine
is ever perfect,
so fine-tunes compulsively.
When he talks about lifters
and rods and bearings
and plugs and valves,
it sounds like jargon,
but it could be incantation.
He is part magician.

When It's Time to Settle Down

I want to be buried
in the corduroy shirt
my children gave me for Christmas.
The river is about the same shade
of green today as the shirt.
Despite the January gloom
five geese are flying northward.
The shirt is comfortable,
not that it could matter.
Somebody will probably wash
my hair and trim my beard
and stick me in a suit.
I have tried to understand all along,
but nothing much was predictable.
I hope the knot at my neck is not so tight
that I look ill at ease.

In Varia Lectio

I am the doomed chicory
beneath the yellow sign
at the corner of the lot.
I am the black black crow
hopping about in the shade.
I am the plantain the silver
groundhog nibbles at dusk.
I am the silver groundhog.
I am the ruby-throated
hummingbird pulling up short
to examine one of the stars
in the sopping flag.
I am the blonde woman
in the little red car
fixing her bra strap.
I am the yowling catbird.
I am the full moon
glowing behind the trees.
I am the pale petunias.
I am the lightning bug
caught in the spider web,
who still blinks.
I am the Norway maple
infested with carpenter ants.
I am the poison ivy
growing in the hedge.
I am the hedge.
I am the doomed chicory.

In Incuriam

I am probably not Rapunzel.

Sitting on a plank near what passes
for a window here, a rectangle cut
in the corrugated wall, for the air
or whatever it is barely passing through
the expanded metal screen, up where no one
outside would think to look, I'm thinking
about the nut again, a nut I dropped
by accident while taking flange bolts loose.

I am probably not a physicist.

The nut jumped from my fingers,
hit the toe of my work boot
hopped to the edge of the deaerator
tank, and leapt into the void.
It ticked and ricocheted off pipes
and valves and conduit and grating,
maybe a beam, and maybe the wall, telling
more of the story of its erratic flight
with the sound of every new collision.
It might not have reached the floor.

I am probably not Japanese.

What goes on inside the deaerator tank
is what happens in a water clock:
water slowly falling falling falling.
I thought about leaping after
the nut but I knew I could not
prevent it from hitting

~ In Lacrimae ~

whatever it was going to hit
even another person, down below.

I am probably flat, a champion!

A tiny man outside crosses the street.

In Lacrimae

Something about the skiers in neon
trunks and bikinis slicing the river,
spewing rooster tails behind them,
something about the man inside
the pilot house of a tug shoving coal upstream,
his ankles crossed on the instrument panel,
his hands up under his yellow tee shirt
scratching his belly, something about
the silver tree across the river,
whether it's been there all along or not
its leaves curling up, exposing their undersides,
and something about the robin
perched atop the rusting flagpole,
the brass snaps, the limp flag,
and the robin's tiny twitching feet,
and something about the cliff face,
and the slow-moving train going south,
and something about the stretch of rocky shore,
and the way waves roll light across the river,
and the different shades and shapes of green
in the forest clinging to the steep bluff,
and something, always something.

In Dividuo

The orange rooster standing here,
deciding which morsel of slag
among billions in the parking lot
deliberating, deliberating,
keeping one wary eye on me,
and twice stabbing at the ground,
suddenly, suddenly,
one of the last creatures
on this planet you'd expect
to be here at quitting time,
has probably come to town
in the back of a pickup truck.
A few of us are part-time farmers.
More are hunters. For those of us
who are neither, but descended
from both, a rooster is about the same
as a squirrel or a rabbit.

The bright sun might penetrate
the overcast sky, making steam
rolling out of some nearby stack
shine so bright and white
you'd think it had to be harmless,
but that would not indicate
the rooster is here for some reason,
whether he knows it or not
and so are we, so are we.

In Libitum

A morning like this,
the phone ringing at five-thirty,

with moderately good news
—just as the rain lets up—

meaning an hour of peace,
a sweet fragrance coming in the window

on the warm breeze drifting
over us in the tangled bed-clothes,

a cardinal singing outside,
something by Sibelius on the radio,

and you saying you feel "frisky,"
a single morning like this

could ruin a man's life.

In Obliquus Oculus

We drift down from the slag
parking lot early,
not a sideways glance among us,

knowing a filthy American
flag stands atop one of the stoves.
We are not skeptical of anything

except where the money goes.
One of us might wave silently
to another as we give some change

to cheerleaders begging at the gate.
With lunches and laundry bags,
everyone has something important

to think about: the friend's wife
who's afraid she's going blind,
the recent retiree everyone knows

has only a month or so
before he passes away
in quiet desperation,

the seventh boiler repairman
to do so in three years,
whether or not the car will last

the coming winter,
whether or not the son
or the drunken brother

will come to his senses
before he kills somebody,
or what life might have been like

with someone else in charge.

In Mirabilia

Some things probably cannot be said
precisely, how flawless the water has become,
for example, how perfectly it reflects
the finest mist rising out of the forest
looming above it or how the trees manage
to cling to the nearly vertical bluff.
The humid air has a rose tint
nobody mentions,
not the grandmothers out walking,
armed with sticks to ward off dogs,
and not the grandfathers bicycling wobbly by,
which means the sun must be setting.
I wonder if anybody else notices.
Earlier, before rain pushed
turmoil across the river,
ailanthus leaves on this bank,
fronds resembling trilobites in structure,
or silverfish,
stood up shaking and waving in the wind,
like unreasonably jubilant cheerleaders.
Now they tremble.
My father is shrinking.

In Dubio Esse

"I cannot believe my life has happened." -E.K.

The sound of the word
nostalgia has the same shape
as Henry Lantz's rooster

declaring everything it knew
one scratchy syllable at a time,
the same clotted poem every morning

emanating from the black interior
of Henry Lantz's black barn,
which oozed creosote in summers

where the rooster resided
like some vital organ,
or incongruous soul.

What I know now is
what always startled that rooster
was the blossom of another sunrise.

In Hoc Homine
(For Extra Credit)

If an ore train takes a few minutes
to pass over an iron trestle at dusk,
the utterly black bridge transforming
in its length a succession of iambic clanks
into perfect trochees as the wheels of each
hopper come onto one end and go off the other,
shaking the bejesus out of a man who wavers
between thinking he might be the ghost of Hart Crane
about to jump into the orange creek below,
so shallow drowning would have to be a severe act
of will, and remembering, as he watches
a bat's erratic flight around the half white,
half invisible moon floating in the cleft
between two hills, how his wife's knees
open for him, how long will the night last?

In Minas

I might eat all the zinnias in town
some night when no one notices,
the salmon moon riding low
over the ridge across the obsidian river.
I night hunker down and talk baseball
to the groundhogs nibbling plantain,
or theology. If I skip my medication
I might dance down Dresden Avenue,
pausing to kiss the sunflowers bowing their heeds.
I might sleep all day beneath the cedars
rising in the scenic, hillside cemetery,
the river gleaning brightly down below.
I might knock my head against a cathedral
door until I finally get some answers.
I might follow the monarch butterflies
in their grand migration south.
I might climb the barren mulberry tree
to declare a general strike, and I might jump.
I might dive into the glittering river
and surface in another century.
I might catalog the items languishing
in all the dilapidated garages in town.
I might liberate all the expired
blue-and-white license plates I find.
And I might even live to be a hundred.

In Sex Mensibus

The last bronze baseball of the season
will roll to a stop under one of the fifty
forsythia bushes containing the outfield,
and roost there like an egg in winter.
The forsythia will be as lush as possible,
and the willows following the creek
beyond right field will not stir at all
as the orange sun falls from the salmon sky.
We will already remember ourselves inaccurately,
vaguely wishing we had known something how
we will by then, as we settle in for the Series,
imagining what a difference it would make
if we knew we could go out into the chilly night
and a blimp would be there, hovering silently,
or nearly so, and invisibly, behind its reassuring message.

In Corrigenda

Despite the philodendron
falling all over itself
like a green embodiment
of the quiet exuberance
some of us are capable of
sometimes, I try to remember
two things about the Japanese
maple—the way drizzle
endowed it with sparkling
buds one certain morning
this past spring and how
the shadow of branches
and lanes appears on the garage
only sometimes in late afternoon
blessing me with another tree
only sometimes, but for hours.
"The philodendron wants to answer
the phone that no longer rings,"
might be a ridiculous statement
if tendrils were not actually
entangled in the brown cord,
if circumstances were different.

In Disiecta Membra

"Few adults ever know where their liver is until it's too late." - Gore Vidal

The liver is located so close to the brain
the two of them are often mistaken for twins.
What soothes this one afflicts that one,
and preserving either jeopardizes the other.
The kidneys govern by default like Congress.
The stomach throbs and pulses with bureaucracy.
The overriding function of the reproductive organs
has top priority. Despite its low intelligence,
the penis has a strong will, to the point of brutality.
(The uterus is lined with shelves of ancient books.)
Every other body process is subordinate.
The heart works like hell: four rooms and a bath,
where ends can barely be met with no view at all.
The eye is the largest organ; it contains the world.
The spinal column is proof we were meant to be plants.
The lungs censor whatever floats in the air.
The mind produces torment as if it were a hormone,
but is itself illusory, a phenomenon of the brain
as insubstantial as a promise. The rest is offal:
the pancreas, the spleen, the tongue and the lips.

In Lux et Veritas

In the vacancy between the liquor
store and the closed bar, Elmo
the vegetable man has his harvest
on display for passing traffic,
sunlight glancing fiercely off
all the late tomatoes and a thousand apples.
The roosting pumpkins somehow
absorb the light and glow,
while Elmo the Psychic
on the truck radio promises
a lucrative change in careers
to one caller, claims he cured himself
of cancer (through visualization)
to another, predicts relocation,
some unspecified something
wonderful by October 15th,
always some improvement barely
short of unmitigated happiness
to everyone who dials his number,
while Elmo the produce man,
tending tables in the hot afternoon,
shooing the same fly for the hundredth time,
selects a fine tomato and takes a bite,
the seedy juice dribbling down
both sides of his chins.

In Itinerarium

Use your camera to capture
the changing face of Jesus
in the rocks exposed
by landslides across the river.

Depending on the subtle shift
of light and shadows in the afternoon,
you may recognize Karl Marx instead,
or even some long gone family member.

Foliage alters the face enough
for Rasputin to become Sibelius,
to become some western desperado
wearing a hold-up handkerchief

and looking like he has a migraine.
Some locals claim the phenomenon
is a kind of window in the mountain
where historical figures look out

with longing or in righteousness
or bewilderment. Remember your camera.
You might see Ernest Hemingway.
Many people in town wear costumes.

In Excelsis

"Fortunately there is history if you can find it."
-Jacques Barzun

At the very peak Sammy loved Trish
and sprayed this truth on a bridge abutment
with stolen fluorescent pink paint.

Small pleasure-craft gathered at dark
just downstream from the marina
at the half-moon bend in the river,

their red and green lights bobbing
on the glassy black water,
somebody's CD player blaring "Bolero,"

and the full, apricot moon suspended,
eerily silent above it all in the eastern sky,
almost edible, a gigantic vanilla wafer.

Aerial displays blossomed from the brow of the hill,
opening like sea anemones,
but the brief wave of euphoria,

or whatever it was,
washed away westward,
and we began this melancholy decline.

In Promptu

The coral sun presides
over the swollen horizon
beyond the dowager magnolia.
The artist dressed in black,
wields an indelible marker,
squints at what she's done,
says she's happy with the portrait
blossoming under her hand:
a black-fringed flower in snow.
She will not give the subject a nose,
even a complimentary one
instead of the crooked turnip
he pushes around with his face.
An observer, husband of the artist,
stands nearby. He and the subject
had been talking about walking on water:
how easy the first few steps always are,
how impossible it becomes.
They have a mutual friend who works
where they work and keeps a brick
on a leash and sometimes takes it
in his arms and tickles its belly.
They are quiet now, one more than the other,
the subject trying to be still, watching
the artist work as the sun sinks lower,
all three of them knowing something now,
some exquisite thing they share: breath,
the sun slowly sinking lower and lower.

In Annus Mirabilis

I am sitting on the freezing metal glider
watching half a dozen herring gulls
gliding and fluttering above the green river
flowing backward and gleaming in the freezing sun.

I am sitting on the freezing metal glider
watching past traffic speeding on the river road.

I am watching the river's green ruffled surface
moving against the dominant current beneath
and thinking of the shearing action between them.

I am sitting on the freezing metal glider
in the freezing winter sun glaring a month early.

How will I make it through the coming winter?
One after another, the gulls half dive,
fluttering and swirling like great leaves,
almost straight down, and settle on the river,
the green ruffled river gleaming in the sun.

I am sitting on the freezing metal glider
watching the perfectly white gulls.

In Rus

Are you estranged from us?

Are you established so well in your field you think we cannot root
you out?

Are you the deer deciding against eating the ornamental shrubbery in
front of the mental health clinic?

Are you the lamp whose golden shade glows in the window every
night?

Are you the forest no one hears because your trees are so noisy, always
clamoring?

Are you the road apples dropping from the only horse in the Christmas
parade?

Are you the eleven members of the Dream Makers 4-H club meeting
on the coldest night of the year in the Fairview Grange Hall?

Are you the green river?

Are you the Amish woman reading her poems from her porch to
Gerald Stem standing in the hot Ohio yard?

Are you Gerald Stem returning the favor?

Are you Frank and Kevin posing like a pair of yard flamingos?

Are you escaping notoriety by remaining hidden and silent more than
necessary?

Are you the snow-covered hills, stubbly with bare trees?

Are you the relief pitcher, glorious in your brief appearance at the end
of the game?

In Ultima Ratio

Almost anything at all,
rain changing to snow and back,
the garden gate opening and closing
in the wind all night, or bare ailanthus
branches scratching at the bright crescent moon
almost until dawn, or slabs of ice
shaped like states and provinces
and eastern European countries
slowly twirling downstream,
constituting a variable and fluid geography
only a little more confounding
than the actual science, or even
opposing traffic on a slushy two-lane highway,
or almost anything else, anything at all.

Early Period

Selected Poem

Some whirled and flurried from the sky.
They came to me in the middle of the night,
some silently, some clumsily bumping into things.
They stuck their tongues in my mouth.
Some slunk along the edge of the river bank
like feral cats. Some ran ahead of me,
like those bumpkins in Pamplona.
They flicked their beautiful tail feathers.
They took things personally and sulked or pouted.
They undressed and they got dressed.
They spoke to strangers and took up with them.
Some recovered from one trauma or another.
Some did not. One saved somebody's life.
They fed me. They traveled with me.
They ventured out of the woods
and nibbled dead meat beside the highway.
They whispered in my good ear.
They scuttled down the street
behind cars and muscular pickups.
They got taken in by shysters.
Some went off somewhere to find themselves.
They danced around in skimpy outfits.
Some slowly became themselves,
as if they didn't know what else to do.

There Are No Poems Here

You may examine every syllable
of every knickknack on every shelf,
but you will not find any poems here.
Nor will you find parts of poems,
newly manufactured or scavenged,
nor words that might be assembled
or reassembled into poems in the future.
Anyway, no poems under the bed.
None under the mattress.
No poems in the toilet tank,
the dropped ceiling, the crawlspace.
None in the attic. None in the garage.
No poems buried beneath the patio.
There are no poems here.
If you read these words backward,
you will not find a poem.
There is no poem in the freezer.
There is no poem under the sink.
There are no poems here.
The poems are in a safe place.

Trompe L'Oeil

This poem is not what it seems,
an application of dark ink to a light page
according to principles of organization
that lead to a more or less orderly gathering
of symbols fraught with meaning.
It is actually a white grating of filigree
laid over the black whole of nothing.
It is the emptiness showing through.

Apple Pie

"In order to make an apple pie from scratch, you must first create the universe." -Carl Sagan, *Cosmos*

Earth is the concrete ball
installed in the pea-gravel garden.
The moon is a pitted rubber ball
set nearby. Every now and then,
a fly or some other small insect
will orbit the earth or land on the moon,
as if nothing else in the universe mattered.

Machine Poem

"A poem is a small (or large) machine made out of words."
-William Carlos Williams

CAUTION
Keep your wits about you
while operating this device,
this assembly of myriad ideas
made manifest, this sculpture
of the history of civilization
in the idiom that uses wheel
and axle, inclined plane, screw,
pulley, wedge, and lever as parts
of speech, this device created
according to our own image and likeness.

Nude #7

She presents
the usual parts
in a way that declares
she is more than the sum
of an eye or two, an arm
or two, and a breast or two.

She is not at all
disarranged. Her parts
appear to be
in working order.
What's going on
behind those blue eyes
could be Achilles
dragging Hector's corpse
around the walls of the city.

O

How weary the moon must be
by now, dressing and undressing
for so many lovers over the years,
gazing in bedroom windows,
standing behind winter trees,
hovering above frosted fields,
managing tides, empathizing with potatoes,
climbing every hill in the world,
and skinny-dipping in every pond,
in return for what? Just lip-service?

Swiss Army™ Poem

The only poem you may ever need;
this poem has a corkscrew and
a defibrillator. It has a piece of chocolate,
a compass, dry socks, a change of underwear,
an internet connection, global positioning,
and term life insurance. Such a handy poem!
It has an atropine injector. Carry it with you
everywhere. It's a map of the world,
a radiation detector, an explosives sensor.
An inhaler. Waterproof matches. An umbrella.

In Toto

A man I knew was killed one day at work,
burned in a freak shower of molten slag
that caught him bent at a water fountain,
as if he were a clerk instead of welder,
so somehow safe from death at thirty-nine.
The accident took place on daylight turn,

so news of it flooded afternoon turn.
Death lingered there, distracting us from work,
the evening Bob died, barely thirty-nine
years old, burnt, as I shoveled other slag
and thought. Half his life he was a welder,
twenty years, then at a water fountain,

when thick, orange-hot slag found the fountain,
he died, surprised he had to take his turn.
Did some greater foreman need a welder?
I never talked to Bob, except at work,
never saw him outside the mill, where slag
washed over him when he was thirty-nine.

I should not care that he was thirty-nine
or that he died at a water fountain
suffering that sudden hot splash of slag,
but I should care about his urge to turn
in that awful heat to get back to work,
where he would not be victim, but welder,

for his survival was as welder,
and had nothing to do with thirty-nine.
And it could be another day at work,
and he could avoid the water fountain.

Yes, I should care about his urge to turn
back to his job, despite the bath of slag,

his last gesture, made despite glowing slag.
If I do not remember this welder,
or what I shoveled on afternoon turn,
whenever I encounter thirty-nine,
let me drink from that same water fountain.
I have an idea that it will work.

Wherever I work, there is always slag,
sometimes a fountain, sometimes a welder,
sometimes thirty-nine lines that will not turn.

Middle Period

Signature Poem

Your hand knows the score
of that brief melody
you call your name:

It knows the measures
and sequence of pulls,
pushes, flicks & quivers,
twitches & final taps
as thoroughly as the skater's body
knows the program of triple toe-loops,
salchows, and tiple axels
which put the same trail
on the ice every time.

Your hand, however,
the prima donna,
does not perform well
under too much scrutiny.
Watch too closely
and you ruin the timing,
the perfect choreography
going haywire.
I would not be surprised
to see a different name
come from under my hand
one day. Not [author's name removed] for once,
but Lotus T. Shimerly, instead,
or Shuster T. Milloy,
or Rose Tully Smith!
I might have to change my life,

rearrange the furniture,
maybe invite me to stay the weekend
to get acquainted.

Thunder & Lightning

These two, married forever,
scare the dogs witless when they visit.
One mut hides beneath the end table.
The other two curs curl
and quiver on the couch…

Despite the brood and the bluster
the rumbles & booms
the bolts of brilliance
this marriage was made in heaven.
Who can deny the electricity?

One would never think
of getting between them.
When they dance
across the prairie at night
you could swear they are
the archetypal sermon.

I'd Like to Believe

It's going to be my heart
and I'd like to believe
I've already felt the first
rumors of revolt. I'd like
to believe I will not die
at the hand of some maniac.
I'd like to believe all
the places I've lived are never vacant,
and I'd like to believe Hansel and Gretel
are still managing a candy store
in Greensburg, Pennsylvania,
and whoever lives above that store now
daily use the refrigerator and bed
I left behind, and I'd like to believe somebody
paused this morning in a certain kitchen
and noticed how the cottonwood outside
perfectly frames the golden mountain beyond it.

I'd like to believe somebody else
has set foot in a perfectly white world,
white trees hovering over white rocks
the air white, everything but me frozen,
even the white sky with its dazzling sun,

I'd like to believe I'll see my children
through, just see them through.
I'd like to believe in something.

I'd like to believe I won't see
another crippled man ask a stranger
for a cigarette. I'd like to believe.

My Genius

I kept my genius hidden
in a gunny sack for years,
like a monkey who could talk.
I don't know who suspected,
surely a family member or two,
the odd acquaintance maybe,
any or all three of my close friends.
It's out of the bag, now,
playing around and having fun
like a monkey suddenly set free.

The Fourth of July

The dead are gathered on the hill and not
Invited into town for any fun.
My mother's joined them lately, those we shun
Outside the city limits. (Ruthless clot!)

Tonight anemones will bloom and fade
Hypnotic in the fragrant summer sky.
Yet momentary; license for the eye
Revoked as beauty is fully displayed.

Unless the dead have learned a trick or two,
Some ways to occupy their former space,
Since their confinement to this grassy place:
Erratic memory will have to do.

Let's go and lie beneath the locust trees.
Let's go and listen to cicadas wheeze.

Bump
For Billy Collins

For all the heed anyone takes
the sign might as well say POEM;
it will be a minor annoyance, at worst,
that should unsettle you only a little.

It will not impede your progress
toward whatever Shangri-La
you're cruising for, hell-bent, at 6
headlong MPH over the limit.

A thousand other hazards
that'll pop your hubcaps off, or worse,
lie ahead, but not this hiccup.
This bump is benign, not yet worth fixing.

It's there, though, 500 feet ahead,
like a poem, waiting for you,
in the dead of night, say, unavoidable,
like a deer confusing your headlights

for the opening toward safety.
Scuffs on the pavement,
and dark stains,
tell the pitiful story.

Poems from 1999

Poem, 1999

They whirled and flurried from the sky.
They came to me in the middle of the night,
some silently, some clumsily bumping into things.
They stuck their tongues in my mouth.
Some slunk along the edge of the river bank
like feral cats. Some ran ahead of me
like those bumpkins in Pamplona.
They flicked their beautiful tail feathers.
They took things personally and sulked or pouted.
They undressed and they got dressed.
They spoke to strangers and took up with them.
Some recovered from one trauma or another.
Some did not. One saved somebody's life.
They fed me. They traveled with me.
They ventured out of the woods
and nibbled dead meat beside the highway.
They whispered in my good ear.
They scuttled down the street
behind cars and muscular pickups.
They got taken in by shysters.
Some went off somewhere to find themselves.
They danced around in skimpy outfits.
Some slowly became themselves
as if they didn't know what else to do.

Personal

You are in this poem
whether you like it or not.
It's the least I could do.
You are in this poem
because of something you did
or did not do, something
we need not mention,
whether you recall it or not.
This is your punishment,
and your reward, all the same.

Zen

This thing is not a poem.
It is not even a thing, really,
self-contained but expansive.
It is imperturbable, and so quiet,
it is practically silent.
It does not seek to become
something it is not.
This is only one bead on a string,
one moment, one thing, one poem.

Please Use Other Door

Our advice has nothing to do
with this door's workability
whether it might come unhinged,
for example, and fall on your foot.
It has nothing to do with you
and your social standing, or ours.
It leads to the kitchen of the sky-
blue house that used to be here.
We have removed the handle.

Reveille

My father sleeps like a corpse,
as if his blankets were a shroud,
his good hand in there holding
his dead arm by the wrist,
his mouth the puckered crater
of a volcano going dormant.
He's a canoe stuck in the shallows.
I want to push him away,
but my duty is to wake him.

Division of Labor

They came out of the hills,
surging from the ground
like ants with so much work to do,
following one another along
the trails of ancient pheromones,
developing the syntax of experience,
the grammar of knowledge,
wherever they've gone, these words,
these marvelous inventions
able to carry such astounding weight.

What Remains to Be Seen

The giddy schizophrenic
wearing a ridiculous chicken hat
with expired lottery tickets stuffed in it,
who feels naked until she gets
her clownish eyebrows penciled on,
laughs and dances in the alley
between Indiana and Illinois,
delighted with the fistful of pastel
currency she can use for rent
wherever she happens to land next.

Placebo

It's possible
this will cure
what ails you,
ease your suffering.
It's also possible
this contains nothing
but artificial sweetener,
maybe non-dairy creamer,
It might, as well, be God.

Shuster T. Milloy*

I am not the man I used to be.
Maybe I've become somebody else
who just looks like me.
Snow accumulates on barges passing by
and disappears into the slate river.
It clings to the hillside opposite.
It slowly obliterates my footprints.
It will soon seem as if I were never here at all.

* A ship-making company

Later Poems (2010-2021)

The Poem

It arrived behind my eyes
a bristly vibrating cord
flexing the single muscle of itself
from one temple to the other
pulling tight and sometimes relaxing,
like the pulsing core of a headache
that lingered for the 14 or 15
years I was not worth knowing
as if I had fallen backward off a cliff
and had to crawl and wallow
around in rubble wanting to cry out
but only mumbling or muttering
while I surveyed my own parts,
sorting them and resorting them,
and holding them up to fluorescence
and testing them against each other,
getting rid of one or two, what the hell
is gall anyway, so who needs a bladder
and forcing most of them to work again
walking the Ho Chi Minh highway
mostly south to north across the hillside
because my one leg is two inches shorter,
never mind that foot being two sizes smaller
mindlessly murdering knotweed
for therapy and the satisfaction.
I could do something beautiful
whether anybody else saw it or not
it being better than raising my hand
against any person including me

and determined over the years
that no father worth his own salt
which used to have considerable value
could refuse to grant unqualified mercy
to his own son and still ever be godly
in any way regardless of contrary rumors
and the most revered authority—
period.

Next Thing I Knew

My father told me on the phone
something was wrong with my mother
as if she were like the furnace
or the hot water heater, both of which
also have mysterious innards
that occasionally must be repaired
or replaced or restarted or something,
and maybe I could get her working again
and I should come down except she was not
stricken the way I knew she had to be,
the way her mother once went slack
when I was twelve I think, staying with her
in case something happened which,
of course, it did, the two of us dancing together,
unable to maneuver her into the chair
but dumping her catawampus on the floor
and had dropped down completely dead
or not, dropped but lain back on the bed
with one knee-length hose pulled up
for church and the other balled in her hand,
while my father was out running
some idiotic errand, now forgotten,
for somebody else who is, now forgotten,
so by the time I got there some neighbors
were gathered in ones and twos and hushed
and there was the gurgling rescue truck
its red lights blinking and the medics
or somebody had yanked my mother's corpse
onto the floor to try something and Amy D.
who would eventually leap from the Market

Street bridge on the coldest night of the year
was at the kitchen table smoking cigarettes
and bearing witness. It was a Sunday.

There Toward the End
"The furnace is working most of the time now."
-E.R.K.

We practiced cannibalism to delay
the inevitable for a time. It seemed
reasonable and even prudent I guess
now none of the furnaces contribute
to our ordinary sense of the hideous
reality we cannot quite recall the behemoths
gobbling coke and limestone and sinter
(no, not cinder and purple iron ore pellets)
and periodically spewing fire and spilling
molten orange slag into thimbles on one side
and yellow molten iron and splashing sparks
into the horizontal bottle cars on the other.

From Time to Time

**"Those who cannot remember the past are condemned
to repeat it." -George Santayana**

The *Niña* and the *Pinta* motored down past here
with their sails furled and without the *Santa Maria,*
the hydrilla giving them both conniptions, the sun
not quite shining off their bitumastic black but not
bitumastic hulls you would maybe expect to be
some shade of brown à la Disney studios and once
Washington having spent the night at Yellow Creek
scooted past figuring this and that and taking notes
and Lewis whose first name could not be farther
from the truth came down from Stern says, "beautiful
filthy Pittsburgh" on his way to meet up with Clark,
not to mention the *Delta Queen* or the *Mississippi Queen*
from time to time either way maybe, the calliope fired up
with me just standing there, might as well be an egret.

Music of the Spheres
For A.F.

You know those matryoshka dolls
the ones that fit inside each other,
what if they were balls, an unknown
number of balls not just six or seven
generations of mothers and daughters

This past Monday or Sunday, a tugboat
pushed two barges and six dead tugboats
upriver past here, weird even for somebody
who has seen young George Washington
or at least his boat or one just like it heading
past and another time Lewis on his way
down from Pittsburgh to pick up Clark,
and once for some reason the *Niña* and *Pinta*
but not the *Santa Maria* can anyone say?

Intelligent Design

was going to call this intelligent design,
but its true name is either false spring
or warm or maybe mild spell because today
broken chunks of white ice from somewhere
up above the dam litter the olive green river
in a haphazard and relentless kind
of procession that, crazy as it seems,
exactly matches bolero streaming straight
from the ether through the once miraculous
now common device perched on a corner
of the circular desk if you remember
the old brass rolls inside the black
lacquer jewelry boxes and now the tune
changes to led zeppelin's been a long time
or woohoo the liberated carousel from walk
of life or the red rubber belt with nubbins
plucking all around the mulberry bush
from the teeth of the steel comb inside
the jack in the box

Exegesis

"The whole machinery of our intelligence, our
general ideas and laws, fixed and external objects,
principles, persons, and gods, are so many symbolic,
algebraic expressions." -George Santayana

God is not dead, none of the gods are dead;
they don't die, they reinvent themselves,
take new names, but most of them grow
sort of redundant or obsolete and retire
to puttering around their respective portions
of creation checking in with so and so,
maybe picking up a piece of litter, stopping
at the local bodega for a lottery ticket
when the jackpot swells beyond all reason,
or sitting on a bench in the park talking
about what it was like back in some heyday
when Zeus could pop his daughter Artemis
right out of his amazing forehead.

In Yoshino

The pea size cherries are as big
as they will ever get and half as many
as last year, thanks to the late frost,
thanks to global warming, or maybe
thanks to the holocaust of honey bees
and the tent worms, or whatever
they are, which inhabit their geometric camp;
although they are still just black specks
and the early bird robin hops once, twice
the way they do and peers sideways as if
she can see straight through the planet
jabs and of course gets the worm, gobbles
it whole, hops once twice, and I swear
celebrates with a little staccato something
you'd think more likely to come out
of Woody Woodpecker, depending on
your age and probably national affiliation,
for all I know, but anyway different
from the usual chirp
                            and the morning
is a little on the cool side, especially
in the shade of the tree, but the sun
now just coming over the ridge
along the top of the plastic rattan chair
radiates through both my thin shirts
onto the scarred desert plain that is
the back I've never seen, just when
a runner in a black top and black shorts
like some rebellious daughter of
the Grim Reaper passes by and waves.

Anger Management

A simple contraption for crushing
my neighbor's mostly empty
beer cans one by one by one
skillfully tipping each one off
the shelf into the black leaf bag lining
the bin. The dealer does not want
unclean cat food cans, but you
can hide a few if you peel the flimsy
labels off and smash them completely flat
with a BFH on the small anvil. Having
done it once already, I know pretty
much how to goad my heart to attack.
Next time maybe I will just go with it.

Apostasy

giving up as much as possible
the passive aggressive quest
to know every blessed thing
about every damned thing
the turn signal blinking its heart out
the umpteenth umpteenth umpteenth
time for no good reason who cares
who knows why gladiolus volunteers
make a stand just beneath the thorn apple
at the top of the bank or the dead man's
fingers break through the ground
at the bottom of the dilapidated stairway
to heaven while soldiers make the news
for laying down their arms peeling
off their uniforms and fleeing
when 90% or more of existence
in the form of matter and energy
and god knows what else is unknown
beyond calculations proving Stonehenge
proves itself notwithstanding so-called
philosophers tangled in their semantics
and withstanding them and amateur
theosophers maybe not since the beginning
of time but well before the Romans
thought to extend their sovereignty
beyond seven unremarkable hills
having learned directly from touching
stone itself a plausible explanation of how
and why the pyramids rose up in the shapes
they did without the aid of extraterrestrials
by the way it no longer matters to me
at least right now not to mention

whether or not or how anybody these days
could do the same not knowing what
we supposedly know about this and that
physics and whatnot whatever whatnot,
could be I find I am becoming knotweed
living for the sole sake of ignorant living

Saint Cinderella

So, sitting on my rump
slashing knotweed
on my neighbor's hillside,
what crawls over me
the slightest change
in the stifling heat,
turns out to be a shadow
gliding raggedly down
over the damned foliage;
beneath me, a turkey
vulture I will call Saint
Cinderella for reminding
me of a chore, my penance,
or therapy or suffering,
whatever it really is—
my exercise, my practice.
When midnight strikes,
it strikes without mercy.

Lazarus

should have passed away
ten or twelve years ago
when the paperwork was fresh,
but for some reason did not,
and then half a dozen years later
went as far as letting go
of every fun thing, whether blessed,
or cursed or both or damned,
knowing in my starving brain-heart
the worry sloshing around was somehow
morphing into peace and relief and
even something like satisfaction,
maybe a click or two shy of pleasure,
being something to be said for endorphins
rinsing away your sins and dread.

Busywork

Inhaled a lightning bug straight down,
at least hope it was a lightning bug,
although they must have their own
troubles without having to worry
about being sucked without warning
into some random abyssal bewilderment,
so released the dead man handle to let
the mower stop chewing the jewelweed,
to chew jewelweed another day
if another day should happen to develop
and tottered past the red picnic table lying
on its back like a dog to the truck,
the exact minute the security light blinks
whitely bright overhead to draw moths
out of the night to pitiless delirium.
I did not know I was breathing so hard,
harder than usual for what I was doing.
One thing that can happen when you keep
busy doing things for the sake of doing them
is you scour the anger out of your heart.

Open Season

Solar powered metronome knickknacks tick
back and forth on the kitchen windowsill
the daisy with its two indecisive little bees
back and forth like rockets between Gaza
and Israel, the ladybug and the one big bee
throwing up their leafy arms to false-start
some cheer or celebration or something else,
mindless the blessedly faceless red zinnia
throwing up its army leaves encouraging
whoever sees to scat-scat, scat-scat in all
their unsynchronized plastic happiness
at once chaotic and carefully composed.
They make me hobble crookedly down to the river
alert for poems, however they exist, beseeching
the sky along the way or nibbling grass or
flying from the willow to chide me, especially
any one of those who populate the river itself
who might surge from their native element
for the quick second of being extraordinary.

Maybe

it all makes sense, the leaves slanting more
or less down toward a grey Heron spookily
just standing there beneath the deformed willow
in water six inches deep exactly where it was not
less than half a minute ago—its elegant neck
and the perfect reflection of its elegant neck
forming an open heart or a heart open at the top
not moving anything at all but, I guess, its two eyes,
although I did think of bringing binoculars
with me in case something...but thinking
nothing, did not. Something stabs the heart,
swallows a gulp whatever it is occurs to me
about the size or so, maybe could be a crayfish
which do inhabit the infestation of hydrilla
two more gulps and finished before I know it.

the heron takes one deliberate step calculating
everything it can: angles-degrees-speed-depth-
probabilities, even its position and location
in the little universe it knows the meal being
whatever it might be in the details, an overload
in the stern the person using the motor to steer
johnboat its bow up out of the water—too much
unintelligible commotion for the heron
departing.

Do Not Resuscitate

shaking more than usual,
not just the bolt in the vibratory
sweet spot at the bottom left handle,
leg wrapped once with duct tape
to thicken the threads tight,
but also a flap under the gas cap
and more wound around holding
the dust cover on the air cleaner
inside the plastic compartment
with three square mouths

rock the block some, in case,
and discover why the wobble
two out of three motor mount bolts
coming loose pull off the plug
wire which goes without saying
draw the two loose bolts tight,
check the third one, lay the whole
shebang back on all fours,
give it a swallow of motor oil, slap
the plug wire back on, yank the cord

starts right up, make one pass down
the hill, hope for the best to last out
the end of the year, sounds better
shut it off to throw a chunk of brick
onto the designated pile of rubble,
pull the cord, something gives out,
sounds like sprocket teeth clacking,
strip it down to the bare motor
plastic and steel for the scrap dealer,
the bag & a small pile of doodads.

Never Ending

It also comes to me pushing
the mower round and round
the cherry tree—maybe Sisyphus
was an ordinary damned poet
having to physically argue
that boulder up the hill over
and over at some point idiotic,
yes, but necessary, never mind
his aching back and his limp.

Again

It comes to me crab walking
the mower closer to the line
of bricks and concrete chunks
improvising a border halfway
up or down the riverbank
depending on your outlook
a discombobulated grasshopper
righting itself and leaping away
from the incomprehensible
contraption bearing down,
never mind the clumsy landing.

Somebody I Know

used to keep what little genius
he had like a rhesus monkey
inside a gunny sack slung over
his shoulder usually asleep
but poking its little head out
here & there, now & then,
according to some theory
of chaos or something being,
of course, a subset of everything
& using him like a dummy, this
being an adequate, if not perfect example.

Hospice

Do not take this as a dire announcement,
but I am now moved into hospice,
still as fine as formerly, so no need
for worry or concern but merely here
for now instead of at the old address. No,

consider this an invitation to visit
me and my so-called condition and
maybe kiss me or not goodbye now
and remember me this way instead
of as a corpse in phony repose displayed

in a satin lined presentation case
which the general plan is to skip anyway.
Please leave your grim expressions and
or somber clothes and consolations at home
for future use and bring your true self or not.

Sudden Glimmer

Whoever she is
she is an apparition,
a sudden reason
to keep going
now that winter
has had its say,
goddess of spring,
whoever she is
in her ordinary dress
nevertheless radiant
bouncing slightly
through the glum
sidewalk crowd
of serious purpose,
whoever she is,
who can explain
this sudden hopefulness
in a weary oldster
stuck in morbid traffic
beginning to move,
not saving anybody's life
whether or not you are here
under the extravagant cherry
on a mild day two weeks before
the last frost date,
before the planting
of the zinnia seeds.

SELECTED HAIKU

a car door—
the way the dog dances
tells me it's you

spring rain—
the gravedigger relatches
the door of his cab

sunny afternoon—
a cortege passes the boy
juggling tangerines

March rain…
something sprouts in a can
on every windowsill

abandoned
high in bare oak branches
yellow paper kite

Memorial Day—
an olive drab sleeping bag
stuffed under the bridge

~ Selected Haiku ~

humid morning—
a hummingbird where the feeder was
last year

heat lightning
flashing on the horizon
fireflies nearby

so many bullfrogs
bellow at the summer pond:
two full moons tonight

toward evening—
a few forsythia petals
on the tractor seat

May day—
the blue gazing globe presides
over the perennials
(for Yu Chang)

late May
my father calls the mockingbird
Frank Sinatra

~ Selected Haiku ~

we stop hammering
but the echoes continue...
geese in the fall sky

first light—
a new batch of mushrooms
on the funeral home lawn

in the time it took
to go inside for iced tea...
the primrose opened

~ Selected Haiku ~

still morning—
the sumac yields
a cardinal

my father's crooked face—
the poppy taking all day
to unfold

spoon-feeding my father
who wants more
once more

~ Selected Haiku ~

distant thunder—
a catbird scraping
the side of his beak

bright sun—
a satellite orbits
the zinnia

noon
the egret shifts from stillness
to stillness

~ Selected Haiku ~

September—
a troop of wild turkeys
crossing the road

frost in the forecast
my neighbor's tomato plants
wearing paper bags

among the sparrows
flitting in the cherry tree—
one blue parakeet

first day
in the country
my hair goes wherever it wants

miserable heat—
talk beneath the camphor tree
turns to mothers-in-law

the preying mantis
in the men's room
watching me watching him

summer evening—
the balcony spider
abides my presence

monarch butterfly
on the painted iris stem
in the waiting room

behind the hay rake
chattering across the field
so many swallows

~ Selected Haiku ~

breathing in
my father's illness
on his birthday

Sunday visit—
clipping my father's fingernails
during the game

mid-December
smoothing my father's cowlick
with my palm

solstice
my father's voice
over the baby monitor

my father's shadow
on the newly painted fence—
autumn beginning

first poppy
the morning my father
passes

abandoned
high in bare oak branches
yellow paper kite

fog mixed with rain
how black are the fenceposts
how green the alfalfa

hidden in marsh grass
the bullfrog bellowing now
gives himself away

fierce sunlight—
a pumpkin vine
venturing onto the sand

the goldfish
make me crave a bowl
of sliced peaches

my brother's birthday
a few licks on the guitar
is all it takes

~ Selected Haiku ~

at the river's edge
ice melts from willow branches—
a dangling fishhook

rush hour—
pigeons in the sculpture garden
walking the way they do

old man with a hose
watering his tomatoes
beside the river

pointing the same way—
shadow of winter's blue spruce
and the weather vane

Christmas Day—
a few extra crumbs
for the goldfish

Snoozles
the little dog knows
I'm toast—

9/15/2021

Jodi and Tim at their Toronto, Ohio home, 2016

Remembrance

By Jodi Dolan Russell

Tim Russell was an American writer who wrote about the everyday happenings and the world of nature that surrounded him, at work in the steel mill and at home with his family. He and I had four children, Shane, Ivan, Violet, and Laurel, and led an extraordinary and vital life in the heart of America.

Tim was the eldest child of Charlie and Ruth (Roush) Russell living in Follansbee, West Virginia, a small steel mill town along the Ohio River. He grew up in a close-knit neighborhood, with his parents often hosting get-togethers. His mom, a homemaker and later a schoolteacher, was known for her baked goods. Charlie, though personable, was a no-nonsense father, with strict household rules. Tim was not allowed to have long hair, yet when discharged from the Army in the 70s, his hair was close to his ears. When Charlie told him, "You'll never amount to anything if you don't cut that hair," Tim vowed to not cut his hair for ten years and did so. In those ten years he had bought a home, had three of his children, obtained his master's degree, and became a published writer.

He was first exposed to the writing world when his high school teacher Walter Wieloh recruited him to help with the school's literary magazine. Later he was more strongly encouraged by college professor, Dr. William Sykes, who recognized his talent and convinced him to change his major from accounting to English. Though highly praised for bringing everyday experience to life, Tim often said he was not interested in fame or fortune, but to simply note his unique observations of the life around him. He would often say "anyone can be a writer." And yet, fellow writers from workshops have shared how he could be disciplined and always demanding of truth.

Tim and I met the summer of 1969 when we were both 18. He had heard that this "cute blonde girl" was at Saint Anthony's Church in Follansbee. I was working then for the Action Corp, a social work program helping Appalachian families then sponsored by the church. Tim showed up and sat behind me at a service, later claiming he fell in love at first sight. I was unaware he existed for a month till he appeared at the school gym playing basketball and clowning around to get my attention. We became good friends. That fall Tim entered West Liberty State College majoring in accounting, and I moved on to Illinois to follow a boy I was interested in. By December, a despondent Tim had dropped out of college to enlist in the Army.

A year later my boyfriend and I had ended it and I was back home in New Jersey. I got a call from Tim at one in the morning. Having received my letter telling him how unhappy I was, he said he would come to rescue me the next day. Much in love, we drove to Pennsylvania where Tim was stationed at a Nike missile base. A short time later, Tim and I were engaged. He received new orders to go to Fort Carson in Colorado Springs, CO. Tim did not want to leave me behind so we decided to marry before he left. At that time written parental approval was needed because we were not 21. On Mother's Day we approached his parents who flatly refused. My family was more open and a couple of months later we were married at Our Lady of Perpetual Help in Oakland, NJ. We celebrated with a modest covered dish reception in my parents' backyard.

The two of us, in our newly purchased Ford Pinto (yet to be paid for), drove all over Colorado - Pike's Peak, Garden of the Gods, Cripple Creek, Cheyenne Mountain. We often stopped at antique stores, tourist sites, and picnicked in the mountains. I had no idea that Tim wanted to be a writer, but at this time, he did begin writing stories. "My Mother Was an Antique", one of his first stories, is based on an old picture we saw in an antique store that bore an uncanny resemblance to his mother. One afternoon we borrowed our landlord's bikes to ride to the south end of Fountain, CO to a tiny, country store where we would go for sodas. Tim spotted a large, wooden, cable spool about 5ft in diameter. He asked if we could have it. We ultimately brought its top with us to West Virginia, and then on to Ohio where Tim used it as a desk in his semi-circle office.

Tim was promoted to Sergea yet resigned in favor of a mill job back home in the Ohio Valley. We were able to purchase a little house a few blocks from the steel mill in Weirton. You could see the mill from our back porch. While working at Weirton Steel as an apprentice millwright, he returned to West Liberty State College where his aunt Angie worked as the school nurse. I shared with Angie the stories and poems Tim had written while in Colorado, and she showed them to the head of the English Department, Dr. William Sykes. He was so impressed with Tim's writing that he summoned him to his office. He asked Tim what his major is and when Tim said accounting, Sykes replied, "Not anymore—it is not. It will now be English." This proves to be a pivotal point in Tim's seeing himself as a writer.

Working at and living so close to the mill, it was impossible not to get swept up in traditions of the mill. An example is what we called "Hoopy Christmas." Annually when bonus checks were given out in the month of July, people celebrated as if it were Christmas. Though Tim was not one to frequent bars, he was enticed by fellow millworkers to meet them at a bar near his home. True to form, taking inspiration from the total of his experiences, he wrote a poem about a man who tried to swing on a ceiling fan that night.

From an early age Tim had a penchant for reading. He devoured information, including a set of encyclopedias from cover to cover. He read books of all genres, the bigger the better, old, new. I recall his reading our young children from *Italian Folktales* by Italo Calvino. He found a thick *Webster's Unabridged Dictionary*, originally published in 1904, containing a supplemental dictionary of foreign words and phrases. Here he noticed Latin phrases with their short definitions which challenged him to use each of these phrases as a title and starting point of a poem—the hundreds of "In…" poems of his work. This was in 1987. He may have been drawn to use Latin as he had served as an altar boy in the Catholic church when Masses were said in Latin and he enjoyed studying Latin in high school.

Over the next fifteen years while living in West Virginia, Tim dove into the writing world, entering many contests, attending writing conferences, and joining local writing groups. Always a charismatic storyteller, Tim would hold people's attention most anywhere, particularly at family gatherings and parties with friends. At the dinner table each night, he would recount daily mill antics and childhood adventures, much to the delight of his family. Tim would keep his rejection slips in a box, which would eventually become boxes. They went from generic form rejections to rejection slips with only a signature, onto rejection letters with signed notes. He persevered in sending and resending. His book *Adversaria* was sent out and rejected eleven times. When he sent it out for the 12th and final time, he showed me the envelope, which I kissed for good luck, and subsequently it won the Terrence Des Pres Prize for Poetry and publication by Tri-Quarterly Books. National recognition followed, and Tim accepted it and hesitantly went out on a reading series to universities, bookstores, and libraries.

Unfortunately, soon after Tim attained publishing success, his health began to deteriorate due to a long-term chronic illness thought to be lupus, so much so that his writing had to take a back seat. He did continue to write, but not at the same pace. In 1994 Tim was forced to retire from the steel mill due to disability, and yet with free time he began to travel some and focus more on writing haiku. One of the first places he traveled was to Port Townsend, Washington, where he was accepted for residency with the Port Centrum Artist Residency Program. I flew out with him to get him settled in for a month. His visit there culminated with the annual Port Townsend Writers Conference. In 1999 he would travel to Japan after winning the 4th Shiki International Haiku contest.

We also traveled to California and to Canada for haiku conferences. At one International Haiku Conference in Chicago we took a "ginko walk" by the Chicago River. When we returned, we were asked to write a haiku. Using the skills Tim had taught me over the years, I made my first attempt ever at writing one. We submitted our haiku but had to leave because Tim became ill. When we arrived home in Ohio, our phone was ringing. It was someone from the contest asking if we knew who had won. Of course, I guessed Tim, which she confirmed. "And who do you think won second place?" she asked. I told her I didn't know. "Well, you have," she responded. Tim's haiku was chosen by the American Judge and mine by the Japanese judge. I was elated. Tim, however, jokingly vowed to not take me along to another haiku contest again.

Later we would travel to London, followed the next year by a trip to Paris where we were the typical tourists and had our photo taken in a train station photobooth. Years earlier he had bought me a smaller figurine of "Winged Victory of Samothrace," which I had kept on display in our home. At the Louvre, he knew we would see the original and loved watching my surprised reaction as I stepped around the corner to see how enormous it really was and how she was standing on a boat. Thanks to our daughter Violet, Tim would take one more long trip to Alaska for three weeks in 2002.

Even when Tim wasn't writing as much, he was always playing with words and encouraging others to listen and be more attuned to the world and nature around them. He could write a haiku at a moment's notice, and he loved to pun. Violet reminds me of how he heard the birds conversing. Some of them would ask "Where do you eat?" and others would answer "Burger King." In the height of her teenage years he would refer to Violet as Cleopatra, "the queen of denial." I have an especially fond remembrance of sending him off to work saying, "Bye, You," with him always replying, "Swamp!" His humor helped us survive and is there in all of his writing.

While preparing for this book, combing through old poems, photos, and visiting old memories, we came across a picture of Tim in a canoe on his Ohio river. Our son Ivan mentioned how the picture perfectly reflects the last half of Tim's life "on a journey or adventure that would always end near that river." So many people supported Tim's becoming the writer he wanted to be and was. I know he would be happy to know that more of his work is being put into print and shared. His words will live on for future generations to read and be reminded of the simple yet vital life of a steel worker and all who labor for family and community.

Acknowledgments

For this book, we are indebted to those who donated their support. We thank the many fellow poets who have supported Timothy's writing for decades and the original publishers of these books: *The Possibility of Turning to Salt* (Ohio Poetry Day Association, 1987); *In Dubio* (State Street Press, 1988); *In Medias Res* in *A Red Shadow of Steel Mills* (Bottom Dog Press, 1991); *In Medias* (1991); *What We Don't Know Hurts* (Talent House Press, 1995), *In Lacrimae* (White Eagle Coffee Store Press, 1996). *Adversaria* (TriQuarterly; 1993).

We thank the following magazines for publishing Timothy's poems: *The Acorn, Alms House Sampler, Amelia, Antietam Review, Antenna, Artful Dodge, Battle of Homestead News, Beloit Poetry Journal, Best of 1987* (Ohio Poetry Day Association), *Best of 1989* (Ohio Poetry Day Association), *Black River Review, Porch, Branch, Cedar Rock, Common Threads, Cincinnati Poetry Review, Circumference, Connecticut River Review, Contemporary Appalachian Poetry, Davidson Miscellany, Dream Shop, Fireweed, 5:am, Free Lunch, Fresh Ground, Gambit, Grab-a-Nickel, Gravity: A Journal of Online Writing, Greenfield Review, Hill & Valley, Hiram Poetry Review, I-West, Kestrel, Independent Review, Laurel Review, Literary Lion, The Little Review* (Weirton Madonna High School), *Listening Eye, Louisville Review, Mad Poets Review, Meklar & Diehl, Mending Wall, Mid-American Review, Minetta Review, Muse, Mountain Pathways, Orpheus, Paperwork, Pavement Saw, Pearl, Pennsylvania Review, Penumbra, Pittsburgh & Tri-State Area Poets, Poetic Page, Poetry, Poetry Northwest, Poetry Now, Poets' Ink, Porch, Raccoon, Riverwind, River City Review, Seneca Review, Shorelines, Solo Flyer, Southern Poetry Review, Sulfur River, Sun Dog, Sunrust, Tendril, Venue, Verve, West Branch, West End, What the Mountains Yield, Wild Wonderful West Virginia, Yarrow, Yellow Jacket, Zuzu's Petals.*

We thank the following publications for sharing Timothy Russell's haiku: *black bough, Brussels Sprout, Central Maryland, Cicada, Common Threads, Dream Shop, dreams wander, Frogpond, Gathering Light, Geppo, Gin Bender, Haijinx, The Haiku Calendar, Haiku Diary, Haiku Headlines, Hastings House, Heron Quarterly, How to Write and Publish Poetry, Japanophile, Kaji Aso, Koan, Lilliput Review, Lotus, My Neighbor's Life, Northern Lights, One Breath, Paper Wasp, Parnassus Literary Journal, Penumbra, Pocket Poems, Point Judith Light, Potpourri , Raw Nervz, Rhyme Time, Sandcutters, A Shadowed Path, Still, Still Life with Stars, Taoism & Poetry Anthology, Timepieces, Verseweavers, When Butterflies Come, Woodnotes, Yellow Moon,*

Words from Timothy Russell

That play between Nature and industry was unavoidable for me. That's the way my world appears. And, if I'm just taking objective notes without any value judgment, then half of the things I write about are going to be industry, and roughly half are going to be natural, because that's what I see when I walk out the door.

Yes, nature is a presence, a comfort…but the natural world in my mind is closer to my home. I mean that's where the poppies grow and that's where I see the orioles. I don't see them flying through the mill…so that's where the comfort of nature is; it's being home and comfortable and safe. And for that half of my life in the mill those natural things are rarely there…except maybe the deer walking on the island.

People I work with have lives outside of the mill. The same way I spend my time writing poetry, some of them run bars, tend farms… they have lives, they're people.

All the Latin titles are phrases that start with "In…" and in a certain way they are all "In Weirton" where I was living. Each one is a different aspect of the same area that I live in

Once I learned that a lyric rant could be considered, or actually was, poetry [from Walt Whitman, Allen Ginsberg, Gerald Stern] then that was freedom for me. Cause then I knew that in writing you have to say what is on your mind. You have to say what you know.

(from *The Writers Forum* video interview with Stan Rubin, 1995)

Chief Contributors

Marc Harshman is the seventh Poet Laureate of West Virginia and an author of more than 14 award-winning books for children. His most recent books of poetry are *Dark Hills of Home* and *Woman in Red Anorak*. He and his wife, Cheryl, live in Wheeling, West Virginia.

Larry Smith is a native of the Ohio Valley and director of Bottom Dog Press and Bird Dog Publishing. He is the author of books of fiction, memoir, and poetry and a professor emeritus of Bowling Green State University. His recent book of poems is *Mingo Town and Memories*. He and his wife Ann live in along the lake in Huron, Ohio.

Ivan Russell has worked many jobs including generator mechanic, broadcast journalist, print journalist, insurance agent and administrative assistant. He currently lives and works in Pittsburgh, often driving past the confluence of the mighty Ohio River, which inspired his father Tim. He considers himself fortunate to provide insight to the editors as a direct addressee of many of Tim's works.

Jodi Russell is an excellent photographer and baker. Busy as a grandmother, she lives on in Toronto, Ohio, and works at an area restaurant. She is an avid gardener, belonging to the Wheeling Herb Society, in Wheeling, West Virginia. She is also in the Dillonvale and the Woodland garden clubs and belongs to The Questers, Hetty Elizabeth Beatty chapter, in Steubenville, Ohio.

Bottom Dog Press Books

In Plena Vita—The Full Life by Timothy Russell, 280 pgs. $20
Hope as a Construction, by David J. Adams, 190 pgs., $18
Green-Silver and Silent: Poems by Marc Harshman 90 pgs., $16
The Thick of Thin: A Memoir by Larry Smith, 238 pgs, $18
Baltic Amber in a Chest: Poems, by Clarissa Jakobsons, 104 pgs., $16
Choices: Three Novellas by Annabel Thomas, 176 pgs., $18
The Pears by Larry Smith 62 pgs. $12
Without a Plea: Poems by Jeff Gundy 96 pgs. $16
What Burden Do Those Trains Bear Away, by Kathleen Burgess $16
Taking a Walk in My Animal Hat, by Charlene Fix, 90 pgs, $16
Earnest Occupations by Richard Hague, 200 pgs, $18
Crows in the Jukebox: Poems, by Mike James, 106 pgs, $16
Portrait of the Artist as a Bingo Worker. by Lori Jakiela, 216 pgs, $18
Cold Air Return: Novel by Patrick Lawrence O'Keeffe, 390 pgs, $20
Flesh and Stones: A Memoir by Jan Shoemaker, 176 pgs, $18
Waiting to Begin: A Memoir by Patricia O'Donnell, 166 pgs, $18
Both Shoes Off: Poems by Jeanne Bryner, 112 pgs, $16
Abandoned Homeland: Poems by Jeff Gundy, 96 pgs, $16
On the Flyleaf: Poems by Herbert Woodward Martin, 106 pgs, $16
The Harmonist at Nightfall: Poems by Shari Wagner, 114 pgs, $16
Ariadne & Other Poems by Ingrid Swanberg, 120 pgs, $16
The Search for the Reason Why: Poems by Tom Kryss, 192 pgs, $16
Kenneth Patchen: Rebel Poet in America by Larry Smith,
Revised 2nd Edition, 326 pgs, Cloth $28
Selected Correspondence of Kenneth Patchen,
Ed.ited with introduction by Allen Frost, Paper $18/ Cloth $28
Awash with Roses: Collected Love Poems of Kenneth Patchen
Eds. Laura Smith and Larry Smith 200 pgs, $16
Maggot: A Novel by Robert Flanagan, 262 pgs, $18
American Poet: A Novel by Jeff Vande Zande, 200 pgs, $18
The Way-Back Room: Memoir of a Detroit Childhood
by Mary Minock, 216 pgs, $18
Echo: Poems by Christina Lovin 86 pgs. $16

Bottom Dog Press http://smithdocs.net
Lsmithdog@smithdocs.net